How to Start an Export Business

A Step By Step Guide to Exporting

By Meir Liraz

Published by BizMove
www.bizmove.com

ISBN: 9781090334015

Table of Contents

a. Excel Financial Projections Creator - simply type in your business' details and assumptions and it will automatically produce a comprehensive set of financial projections for your specific business, including: Start-Up Expenses, Projected Balance Sheet, Projected Cash Flow Statement, Financial Ratios Analysis, Projected Profit and Loss Statement, Break Even Analysis, and more.

b. Detailed guide that will walk you step by step and show you exactly how to effectively use the above Excel Financial Projections Creator.

c. How to Improve Your Leadership and Management Skills (eBook) - Discover powerful strategies to motivate and inspire your people to bring out the best in them. Be the boss people want to give 200 percent for.

d. Small Business Management: Essential Ingredients for Success (eBook) - Learn effective business management tricks, secrets and shortcuts to make your business a success.

1. Introduction to Exporting

This guide will walk you step by step through all the essential phases of starting a successful export based business There is profit to be made in export. The international market is much larger than the local market. Growth rates in many overseas markets far outpace domestic market growth. And meeting and beating innovative competitors abroad can help companies keep the edge they need at home.

There are also real costs and risks associated with export data. It is up to each company to weigh the necessary commitment against the potential benefit.

Do you need export data?: Ten important recommendations for successful exporting should be kept in mind:

Obtain qualified export counseling and develop a master international marketing plan before starting an export business. The plan should clearly define goals, objectives, and problems encountered.

Secure a commitment from top management to overcome the initial difficulties and financial requirements of exporting. Although the early delays and costs involved in exporting may seem difficult to justify in comparison with established domestic sales, the exporter should take a long-range view of this process and carefully monitor international marketing efforts.

Take sufficient care in selecting overseas distributors. The complications involved in overseas communications and transportation require international distributors to act more independently than their domestic counterparts.

Establish a basis for profitable operations and orderly growth. Although no overseas inquiry should be ignored, the firm that acts mainly in response to unsolicited trade leads is trusting success to the element of chance.

Devote continuing attention to export business when the local market booms. Too many companies turn to exporting when business falls off in the domestic market. When domestic business starts to boom again, they neglect their export trade or relegate it to a secondary position.

Treat international distributors on an equal basis with domestic counterparts. Companies often carry out institutional advertising campaigns, special discount offers, sales incentive programs, special credit term programs, warranty offers, and so on in the domestic market but fail to make similar offers to their international distributors.

Do not assume that a given market technique and product will automatically be successful in all countries. What works in Japan may fall flat in Saudi Arabia. Each market has to be treated separately to ensure maximum success.

Be willing to modify products to meet regulations or cultural preferences of other countries. Local safety and security codes as well as import restrictions cannot be ignored by foreign distributors.

Print service, sale, and warranty messages in locally understood languages. Although a distributor's top management may speak English, it is unlikely that all sales and service personnel have this capability.

Provide readily available servicing for the product. A product without the necessary service support can acquire a bad reputation quickly.

2. How to Plan and Start Your Export Business

The purpose of this chapter is to teach you exactly how to prepare your business to enter the international marketplace. This is a step-by-step guide that will lead you through the process of exporting your product to an international market. The worksheet is divided into sections.

Each section of the export business plan must be completed before you start the next section. After you have completed the entire worksheet, you will be ready to develop an international business plan to export your product. Once the business plan is completed, an in-depth analysis of your readiness to export can be completed.

Products/Services

STEP 1: Select the most exportable products to be offered internationally.

STEP 1: Select the most exportable products to be offered internationally.

STEP 1: Select the most exportable products to be offered internationally.

To identify products with export potential for distribution internationally, you need to consider products that are successfully distributed in the domestic market. The product needs to fill a targeted need for the purchaser in export markets according to price, value to customer/country and market demand.

What are the major products your business sells?

1. _____

2. _____

3. _____

What products have the best potential for international trade?

1. _____

2. _____

STEP 2: Evaluate the products to be offered internationally.

What makes your products unique for an overseas market?

1. _____

2. _____

3. _____

Why will international buyers purchase the products from your company?

1. _____

2. _____

3. _____

How much inventory will be necessary to sell overseas?

1. _____

2. _____

3. _____

Identifying Products With Export Potential

List below the products you believe have export potential. Indicate the reasons you believe each product will be successful in the international marketplace.

Products/Services / Reasons for Export Success

1. _____

2. _____

3. _____

4. _____

5. _____

Decision Point: These products have export potential:

_____

_____

_____

_____

Planning

What is the purpose of completing this workbook?

You know that you want to see your company grow through exporting.

Five reasons it will be worth your time and effort:

Careful completion of this workbook will help evaluate your level of commitment to exporting.

The completed workbook can help you evaluate your product's potential for the international trade market.

The workbook gives you a tool to help you better manage your international business operations successfully.

The completed workbook will help you communicate your business ideas to persons outside your business and can be an excellent starting point for developing an international financing proposal.

Businesses managed are more successful when working from a business plan.

Can't I hire someone to do this for me?

No! Nobody will do your thinking or make decisions for you. This is your business. If the business plan is to be useful, it must reflect your ideas and efforts - not those of an outsider.

Why is planning so important?

The planning process forces you to look at your future business operations and anticipate what will happen. This process better prepares you for the future and makes you more knowledgeable about your business. Planning is vital for marketing your product in an international marketplace.

Any firm considering entering into international business transactions must understand that doing business internationally is not a simple task nor one for the faint of heart. It is stimulating and potentially profitable in the long-term but requires much preparation and research prior to the first transaction.

In considering products for the international market, a business needs to be:

Successful in its present domestic operation.

Willing to commit its resources of time, people and capital to the program. Entry into the international market may take as long as two years to generate profit with cash outflow during that period.

Sensitive and aware of the cultural implications of doing business internationally.

Developing a business plan helps you assess your present market situation, business goals, and commitment which will increase your opportunities for success.

What's the bottom line for me if I do the plan?

Research shows that small business failure rates among new businesses are significantly lower for new businesses that have developed a business plan.

Isn't planning just for the big companies?

Planning is important for any organization that wants to approach the future with a plan of action. The future comes whether you are prepared for it or not. A business plan helps you anticipate the future and make well-informed decisions because you have thought about the alternatives you will be facing.

How often do I have to do this?

A plan must be revised as needed, at least once a year. Planning is a continuous process. You will be surprised how much easier it is to develop a business plan after the first time. Plus, after a revision or two you will know more about your international business market opportunities to export products.

Goal Setting

Determining your business goals can be a very exciting and often challenging process. It is, however, a very important step in planning your entry into the international marketplace. The following exercise is intended to help you clarify your short and long-term business goals.

STEP 1: Define long-term goals.

A) What are your long-term goals for this business in the next 5 years? Examples: increase export sales by ___% annually; develop country cultural profiles.

B) How will the international trade market help you reach your long-term goals?

STEP 2: Define short-term goals.

A) For your international business, what are your first year goals? Examples: attend export seminars, select a freight forwarder.

B) What are your two-year goals for your international business products/services?

STEP 3: Develop an action plan to reach your short-term goals by using international trade.

STEP 3: Develop an action plan to reach your short-term goals by using international trade.

STEP 3: Develop an action plan to reach your short-term goals by using international trade.

STEP 3: Develop an action plan to reach your short-term goals by using international trade.

Industry Analysis

STEP 1: Determine your industry's growth for the next 3 years.

STEP 1: Determine your industry's growth for the next 3 years.

STEP 1: Determine your industry's growth for the next 3 years.

STEP 1: Determine your industry's growth for the next 3 years.

Talk to people in the same business or industry, research industry-specific magazines, attend trade fairs and seminars.

STEP 2: Research how competitive your industry is in the global markets.

STEP 3: Find out your industry's future growth in the international market.

STEP 4: Research government market studies that have been conducted on your industry's potential international markets.

STEP 5: Find export data available on your industry.

STEP 2: Research how competitive your industry is in the global markets.

STEP 3: Find out your industry's future growth in the international market.

STEP 4: Research government market studies that have been conducted on your industry's potential international markets.

STEP 5: Find export data available on your industry.

STEP 2: Research how competitive your industry is in the global markets.

STEP 3: Find out your industry's future growth in the international market.

STEP 4: Research government market studies that have been conducted on your industry's potential international markets.

STEP 5: Find export data available on your industry.

STEP 2: Research how competitive your industry is in the global markets.

STEP 3: Find out your industry's future growth in the international market.

STEP 4: Research government market studies that have been conducted on your industry's potential international markets.

STEP 5: Find export data available on your industry.

Your business/Company Analysis

STEP 1: Why is your business successful in the domestic market? What's your growth rate?

STEP 2: What products do you feel have export potential?

STEP 3: What are the competitive advantages of your products or business over other domestic and international businesses?

Pros and Cons of Market Expansion

Brainstorm a list of pros and cons for expanding your market internationally. Based on your product and market knowledge, determine your probability of success in the international market.

Industry/Product:

Pros / Cons

1.

2.

3.

4.

5.

6.

Probability of Success

0% _____ 25% _____ 50% _____ 75% _____ 100% _____

Marketing Your Product

Given the market potential for your products in international markets, how is your product unique?

1. What are your product's advantages?

2. What are your product's disadvantages?

3. What are the competitive product's advantages?

4. What are the competitive product's disadvantages?

What are the needs that will be filled by your product in a foreign market? What competitive products are sold abroad and to whom?

How complex is your product? What skills or special training are required to:

1. Install your product?

2. Use your product?

3. Maintain your product?

4. Service your product?

What options and accessories are available?

1. Has an after-market been developed for your product?

2. What other equipment does the buyer need to use your product?

3. What complementary goods does your product require?

If your product is an industrial good:

1. What firms are likely to use it?

2. What is the useful life of your product?

3. Is use or life affected by climate? If so, how?

4. Will geography affect product purchase, for example transportation problems?

5. Will the product be restricted abroad, for example tariffs, quotas or non-tariff barriers?

If the product is a consumer good:

1. Who will consume it? How frequently will the product be bought?

2. Is consumption affected by climate?

3. Is consumption affected by geography, for example transportation problems?

4. Will the product be restricted abroad for example tariffs, quotas or non-tariff barriers?

5. Does your product conflict with traditions, habits or beliefs of customers abroad?

STEP 1:

Select the best countries to market your product.

Since the number of world markets to be considered by a company is very large, it is neither possible nor advisable to research them all. Thus, your firm's time and money are spent most efficiently by using a sequential screening process.

The first step in this sequential screening process for the company is to select the more attractive countries for your product. Preliminary screening involves defining the physical, political, economic and cultural environment. Rate the following market factors in each category.

(1) Select 2 countries you think have the best market potential for your product;

(2) Review the market factors for each country;

(3) Research data/information for each country;

(4) Rate each factor on a scale of 1-5 with 5 being the best; and

(5) Select a target market country based on your ratings

MARKET FACTOR ASSESSMENT Country A Country B

Demographic/Physical Environment:

Population size, growth, density

Urban and rural distribution

Climate and weather variations

Shipping distance

Product-significant demographics

Physical distribution and communication network

Natural resources

Political Environment:

System of government

Political stability and continuity

Ideological orientation

Government involvement in business

Attitudes toward foreign business

(trade restrictions, tariffs, non-tariff barriers, bilateral trade agreements)

National economic and developmental priorities

Economic Environment:

Overall level of development

Economic growth:

GNP, industrial sector

Role of foreign trade in the economy

Currency:

inflation rate, availability, controls, stability of exchange rate

Balance of payments

Per capita income and distribution

Disposable income and expenditure patterns

Social/Cultural Environment:

Literacy rate, educational level

Existence of middle class

Similarities and differences in relation to home market

Language and other cultural considerations

Market Access, Limitations on trade:

high tariff levels, quotas

Documentation and import regulations

Local standards, practices, and other non-tariff barriers

Patents and trademark protection

Preferential treaties

Legal considerations for investment

taxation, repatriation, employment, code of laws

Product Potential:

Customer needs and desires

Local production, imports, consumption

Exposure to and acceptance of product

Availability of linking products

Industry-specific key indicators of demand

Attitudes toward products of foreign origin

Competitive offerings

Local Distribution and Production:

Availability of intermediaries

Regional and local transportation facilities

Availability of manpower

Conditions for local manufacture

Indicators of population, income levels and consumption patterns should be considered. In addition, statistics on local production trends, along with imports and exports of the product category, are helpful for assessing industry market potential. Often, an industry will have a few key indicators or measures that will help them determine the industry strength and demand within an international market. A manufacturer of medical equipment, for example, may use the number of hospital beds, the number of surgeries and public expenditures for health care as indicators to assess the potential for its products.

What are the projected growth rates for the two countries selected over the next 3-5 years?

STEP 2:

Determine Projected Sales Levels

What is your present domestic market percentage?

What are the projected sales for similar products in your chosen international markets for the coming year?

What sales volume will you project for your products in these international markets for the coming year?

What is the projected growth in these international markets over the next five years?

STEP 3:

Identify Customers Within Your Chosen Markets

What companies, agents or distributors have purchased similar products?

What companies, agents or distributors have made recent requests for information on similar products?

What companies, agents or distributors would most likely be prospective customers for your export products?

STEP 4:

Determine Method Of Exporting

How do other domestic firms sell in the markets you have chosen?

Will you sell direct to the customer?

Who will represent your firm?

Who will service the customer's needs?

STEP 5:

Building A Distributor or Agent Relationship

Will you appoint an agent or distributor to handle your export market?

What facilities does the agent or distributor need to service the market?

What type of client should your agent or distributor be familiar with in order to sell your product?

What territory should the agent or distributor cover?

What financial strength should the agent or distributor have?

What other competitive or non-competitive lines are acceptable or not acceptable for the agent or distributor to carry?

How many sales representatives does the agent or distributor need and how often will they cover the territory?

Will you use an export management company to do your marketing and distribution for you?

If yes, have you developed an acceptable sales and marketing plan with realistic goals you can agree to?

Comments:

Support Functions

To achieve efficient sales offerings to buyers in the targeted markets, several concerns regarding products, literature and customer relations should be addressed.

STEP 1:

Identify product concerns.

Can the potential buyer see a functioning model or sample of your product that is substantially the same as would be received from production?

Comments:

What product labeling requirements must be met? (Metric measurements, AC or DC electrical, voltage, etc.) Keep in mind that the European Community now requires 3 languages on all new packaging.

When and how can product conversion requirements be obtained?

Can product be delivered on time as ordered?

Comments:

_____

STEP 2:

Identify literature concerns.

If required, will you have literature in language other than English?

Do you need a product literature translator to handle the technical language?

What special concerns should be addressed in sales literature to ensure quality and informative representation of your product?

STEP 3:

Identify customer relations concerns.

What is delivery time and method of shipment?

What are payment terms?

What are the warranty terms?

Who will service the product when needed?

How will you communicate with your customer? through a local agent or fax?

Are you prepared to give the same order and delivery preference to your international customers that you give to your domestic customers?

Marketing Strategy

In international sales, the chosen "terms of sale" are most important.

Where should you make the product available: at your plant, at the port of exit, landed at the port of importation or delivered free and clear to the customer's door? The answer to this question involves determining what the market requires, and how much risk you are willing to take.

Pricing strategy depends on "terms of sale" and also considers value-added services of bringing the product to the international market.

STEP 1:

Define International Pricing Strategy.

How do you calculate the price for each product?

What factors have you considered in setting prices?

Which products' sales are very sensitive to price changes? How important is pricing in your overall marketing strategy? What are your discount policies?

What terms of sales are best for your export product?

STEP 2:

Define promotional strategy

What advertising materials will you use?

What trade shows or trade missions will you participate in, if any?

What time of year and how often will foreign travel be made to customer markets?

STEP 3:

Define customer services

What special customer services do you offer?

What types of payment options do you offer?

How do you handle merchandise that customers return?

Sales Forecast

Forecasting sales of your product is the starting point for your financial projections. The sales forecast is extremely important, so it is important you use realistic estimates. Remember that sales forecasts show the expected time the sale is made. Actual cash flow will be impacted by delivery date and payment terms.

Step 1: Fill in the units-sold line for markets 1, 2, and 3 for each year on the following worksheet.

Step 2: Fill in the sales price per unit for products sold in markets 1, 2 and 3.

Step 3: Calculate the total sales for each of the different markets (units sold x sales price per unit).

Step 4: Calculate the sales (all markets) for each year - add down the columns.

Step 5: Calculate the five year total sales for each market - add across the rows.

SALES FORECASTS - FIRST FIVE YEARS

	1	2	3	4	5
Market 1					
Units Sold	____	____	____	____	____
Sale Price/Unit	____	____	____	____	____
Total Sales	____	____	____	____	____
Market 2					
Units Sold	____	____	____	____	____
Sale Price/Unit	____	____	____	____	____
Total Sales	____	____	____	____	____
Market 3					
Units Sold	____	____	____	____	____
Sale Price/Unit	____	____	____	____	____
Total Sales	____	____	____	____	____
Total Sales	____	____	____	____	____
All Markets	____	____	____	____	____

COST OF GOODS SOLD

The cost of goods sold internationally is partially determined by pricing strategies and terms of sale. To ascertain the costs associated with the different terms of sale, it will be necessary to consult an international freight forwarder. For example, a typical term of sale offered by a domestic exporter is cost, insurance and freight (CIF) port of destination. Your price includes all the costs to move product to the port of destination.

A typical cost work sheet will include some of the following factors. These costs are in addition to the material and labor used in the manufacture of your product: export packing, forwarding, container loading, documentation, inland freight, consular legalization, truck/rail unloading, bank documentation, wharfage, dispatch, handling, bank collection fees, terminal charges, cargo insurance, ocean freight, other misc., bunker surcharge, courier mail.

To complete this worksheet, you will need to use data from the sales forecast. Certain costs related to your terms of sale may also have to be considered.

Step 1: Fill in the units-sold line for market 1, 2, and 3 for each year.

Step 2: Fill in the cost per unit for products sold in markets 1, 2, and 3.

Step 3: Calculate the total cost for each of the products - (units sold x cost per unit).

Step 4: Calculate the cost of goods sold - all products for each year - add down the columns.

Step 5: Calculate the five-year cost of goods for each market - add across the rows.

COST OF GOODS SOLD - FIRST FIVE YEARS

	1	2	3	4	5
Market 1					
Units Sold	___	___	___	___	___
Sale Price/Unit	___	___	___	___	___
Total Cost	___	___	___	___	___
Market 2					
Units Sold	___	___	___	___	___
Sale Price/Unit	___	___	___	___	___
Total Cost	___	___	___	___	___
Market 3					
Units Sold	___	___	___	___	___
Sale Price/Unit	___	___	___	___	___
Total Cost	___	___	___	___	___
Cost of Goods Sold All Markets	___	___	___	___	___

INTERNATIONAL OVERHEAD EXPENSES

To determine overhead costs for your export products, you should be certain to include costs that pertain only to international marketing efforts. For example, costs for domestic advertising of service that do not pertain to the international market should not be included. Examples of most typical expense categories for an export business are listed on the next page. Some of these expenses will be first year start-up expenses, and others will occur every year.

Step 1: Review the expenses listed on the next page. These are expenses that will be incurred because of your international business. There may be other expense categories not listed - list them under "other expenses."

Step 2: Estimate your cost for each expense category.

Step 3: Estimate any domestic marketing expense included that is not applicable to international sales.

Step 4: Calculate the total for your international overhead expenses.

EXPENSE	COST			
	Market 1	Market 2	Market 3	Total Yr 1
Legal Fees	_____	_____	_____	_____
Accounting Fees	_____	_____	_____	_____
Promotional Material	_____	_____	_____	_____
Travel	_____	_____	_____	_____
Communication	_____	_____	_____	_____
Equipment	_____	_____	_____	_____
Advertising Allowances	_____	_____	_____	_____
Promotional Expenses	_____	_____	_____	_____
(e.g., trade shows, etc.)				
Other Expenses	_____	_____	_____	_____
Total Expenses	_____	_____	_____	_____
Less Domestic Expenses	_____	_____	_____	_____
(Included Above, if any)				
Total Intern' Start-up Expenses	_____	_____	_____	_____

PROJECTED INCOME STATEMENT - YEAR 1 to 5, ALL MARKETS

You are now ready to assemble the data for your projected income statement. This statement will calculate your net profit or net loss (before income taxes) for each year.

Step 1: Fill in the sales for each year. You already estimated these figures; just recopy them on the work sheet.

Step 2: Fill in the cost of goods sold for each year. You already estimated these figures, just recopy on the work sheet.

Step 3: Calculate the Gross Margin for each year (Sales minus Cost of Goods Sold).

Step 4: Calculate the Total Operating Expenses for each year.

Step 5: Calculate the Net Profit or Net Loss (Before Income Taxes) for each year (Gross Margin minus Total Operating Expenses).

PROJECTED INCOME STATEMENT - YEAR 1 to 5, ALL MARKETS

	1	2	3	4	5
International Sales	___	___	___	___	___
Cost of Goods Sold	___	___	___	___	___
Gross Margin	___	___	___	___	___
International Operating Expenses:					
Legal	___	___	___	___	___
Accounting	___	___	___	___	___
Advertising	___	___	___	___	___
Travel	___	___	___	___	___
Trade shows	___	___	___	___	___
Promotional Material	___	___	___	___	___
Supplies	___	___	___	___	___
Communication Equipment	___	___	___	___	___
Interest	___	___	___	___	___
Insurance	___	___	___	___	___
Other	___	___	___	___	___
Total Intern' Operating Expenses	___	___	___	___	___

TIMETABLE

This is a worksheet that you will need to work on periodically as you progress in the worksheet. The purpose is to ensure that key tasks are identified and completed to increase the success of your international business.

STEP 1:

Identify key activities

By reviewing other portions of your business plan, compile a list of tasks that are vital to the successful operation of your business. Be sure to include travel to your chosen market as applicable.

STEP 2:

Assign responsibility for each activity

For each identified activity, assign one person primary responsibility for the completion of that activity.

STEP 3:

Determine scheduled start date

For each activity determine the date when work will begin. You should consider how the activity fits into your overall plan as well as the availability of the person responsible.

STEP 4:

Determine scheduled finish date

For each activity determine when the activity must be completed.

ACTION PLAN

STEP 1:

Verify completion of previous pages.

You should have finished all the other sections in the worksheet before continuing any further.

STEP 2:

Identify your business plan audience.

What type of person are you intending to satisfy with this business plan?

The summary should briefly address all the major issues that are important to this person. Keep in mind that this page will probably be the first read by this person. It is extremely important the summary be brief yet contain the information most important to the reader. This section should make the reader want to read the rest of your plan.

STEP 3:

Write a one-page summary.

You will now need to write no more than a page summarizing all the previous work sheets you have completed.

Determine which sections are going to be most interesting to your reader. Write one to three sentences that summarize each of the important sections.

These sentences should appear in the order of the sections of your business plan. The sentences must fit together to form a summary and not appear to be a group of loosely related thoughts.

You may want to have several different summaries, depending on who will read the business plan.

INTERNATIONAL BUSINESS PLAN SUMMARY:

_____

Preparing an Export Price Quotation

Setting proper export prices is crucial to a successful international sales program; prices must be high enough to generate a reasonable profit, yet low enough to be competitive in overseas markets. Basic pricing criteria - costs, market demand, and competition - are the same for domestic and foreign sales. However, a thorough analysis of all cost factors going into a cost, insurance and freight (CIF) quotation may result in prices that are different from domestic ones.

"Marginal cost" pricing is the most realistic and frequently used pricing method. Based on a calculation of incremental costs, this method considers the direct out-of-pocket expenses of producing and selling products for export as a floor beneath which prices cannot be set without incurring a loss. There are important principles that should be followed when pricing a product for export, summarized below.

COST FACTORS

In calculating an export price, be sure to take into account all the cost factors for which you, the exporter, are liable.

1. Calculate direct materials and labor costs involved in producing the goods for export.

2. Calculate your factory overhead costs, prorating the amount of overhead chargeable to your proposed export order.

3. Deduct any charges not attributable to the export operation (i.e., domestic marketing costs, domestic legal expenses), especially if export sales represent only a small part of total sales.

4. Add in the other out-of-pocket expenses directly tied to the export sales, such as:

travel expenses

catalogs, slide shows, video presentations

promotional material

export advertising

commissions

transportation expenses

packing materials

legal expenses*

office supplies*

patent and trademark fees*

communications*

taxes*

rent*

insurance*

interest*

provision for bad debts

market research

credit checks

translation costs

product modification

consultant fees

freight forwarder fees

*These items will typically represent the cost of the total operation, so be sure to prorate these to reflect only the cost of producing the goods for export.

5. Allow yourself a realistic price margin for unforeseen costs, unavoidable risks, and simple mistakes that are common in any new undertaking.

6. Also allow yourself a realistic profit or mark-up.

Other Factors to Consider

Market Demand

Market Demand - As in the domestic market, product demand is the key to setting prices in a foreign market. What will the market bear for a specific product or service? What will the estimated consumer price for your product be in each foreign market? If your prices seem out of line, try some simple product modifications to reduce the selling price, such as simplification of technology or alteration of product size to conform to local market norms. Also keep in mind that currency valuations alter the affordability of goods. A good pricing strategy should accommodate fluctuations in currency.

Competition - As in the domestic market, few exporters are free to set prices without carefully evaluating their competitor's pricing policies. The situation is further complicated by the need to evaluate the competition's prices in each foreign market an exporter intends to enter. In a foreign market that is serviced by many competitors, an exporter may have little choice but to match the going price or even go below it to establish a market share. If, however, the exporter's product or service is new to a particular foreign market, it may be possible to set a higher price than normally charged domestically.

3. How to Sell Overseas

Many successful exporters first started to sell overseas by responding to an inquiry from a foreign firm. Many firms receive such requests annually, but most firms do not become successful exporters. What separates the successful exporter from the unsuccessful exporter? There is no single answer, but often the firm that becomes successful sell overseas knows how to respond to inquiries, can separate the wheat from the chaff, recognizes the business practices involved in international selling, and takes time to build a relationship with the client. Although this may seem to be a large number of factors, they are all related and flow out of one another.

RESPONDING TO INQUIRIES

Most but not all, foreign letters of inquiry are in English. A firm may look to certain service providers (such as banks or freight forwarders) for assistance in translating a letter of inquiry in a foreign language. Most large cities have commercial translators who translate for a fee. Many colleges and universities also provide translation services.

A typical inquiry asks for product specifications, information, and price. Some foreign firms want information on purchasing a product for internal use; others (distributors and agents) want to sell the product in their market. A few firms may know a product well enough and want to place an order. Most inquiries want delivery schedules, shipping costs, terms, and, in some cases, exclusivity arrangements.

Regardless of the form such inquiries take, a firm should establish a policy to deal with them. Here are a few suggestions:

Reply to all correspondents except to those who obviously will not turn into customers. Do not disregard the inquiry merely because it contains grammatical or typographical errors, which may result from the writer knowing English only as a second language. Similarly, if the printing quality of the stationery does not meet usual standards, keep in mind that printing standards in the correspondent's country may be different. Despite first impressions, the inquiry may be from a reputable, well-established firm.

Reply promptly, completely, and clearly. The correspondent naturally wants to know something about your firm before doing business with it. The letter should introduce the firm sufficiently and establish it as a reliable supplier. The reply should provide a short but adequate introduction to the firm, including bank references and other sources that confirm reliability. The firm's policy on exports should be stated, including cost, terms, and delivery.

Enclose information on the firm's goods or services.

When speedy communication is called for, send a fax. Unlike telephone communications, fax may be used effectively despite differences in time zones and languages.

Set up a file for foreign letters. They may turn into definite prospects as export business grows. If the firm has an intermediary handling exports, the intermediary may use the file.

Sometimes an overseas firm requests a pro forma invoice, which is a quotation in an invoice format. It is used rarely in domestic business but frequently in international trade.

SEPARATING THE WHEAT FROM THE CHAFF

How can a firm tell if an overseas inquiry is legitimate and from an established source? A company can obtain more information about a foreign firm making an inquiry by checking with the following sources of information about foreign firms:

Business libraries. Several publications list and qualify international firms, including Jane's Major Companies of Europe, Dun and Bradstreet's Principal International Business, and many regional and country directories.

International banks. Bankers have access to vast amounts of information on foreign firms and are usually very willing to assist corporate customers.

Foreign embassies. The commercial (business) sections of most foreign embassies have directories of firms located in their countries.

Sources of credit information. Credit reports on foreign companies are available from many private sector sources, including Dun and Bradstreet and Graydon International.

BUSINESS PRACTICES IN INTERNATIONAL SELLING

Awareness of accepted business practices is paramount to successful international selling. Because cultures vary, there is no single code by which to conduct business. Certain business practices, however, transcend culture barriers:

Answer requests promptly and clearly.

Keep promises. The biggest complaint from foreign importers about suppliers is failure to ship as promised. A first order is particularly important because it shapes a customer's image of a firm as a dependable or an undependable supplier.

Be polite, courteous, and friendly. It is important, however, to avoid undue familiarity or slang. Some overseas firms feel that the usual brief business letter is lacking in courtesy.

Personally sign all letters. Form letters are not satisfactory.

Before traveling to a new market, the traveler should learn as much about the culture as possible to avoid embarrassing situations. For example, in Mexico it is customary to inquire about a colleague's wife and family, whereas in many Middle Eastern countries it is taboo. Patting a U.S. colleague on the back for congratulations is a common practice, but in Japan it would be discourteous. Clothes, expressions, posture, and actions are all important considerations in conducting international business.

Another important consideration is religious and national holidays. Trying to conduct business on the Fourth of July in the United States would be difficult, if not impossible. Likewise, different dates have special significance in various countries. Some countries have long holidays by our standards, making business difficult. For example, doing business is difficult in Saudi Arabia during the month of fasting before the Ramadan religious festival.

Numerous seminars, film series, books, and publications exist to help the overseas traveler. Try to obtain cultural information from business colleagues who have been abroad or have expertise in a particular market. A little research and observation in cultural behavior can go a long way in international commerce. Likewise, a lack of sensitivity to another's customs can stop a deal in its tracks. Foreign government consulates offer a wealth of information on business customs and norms for their countries.

BUILDING A WORKING RELATIONSHIP

Once a relationship has been established with an overseas customer, representative, or distributor, it is important that the exporter work on building and maintaining that relationship. Common courtesy should dictate business activity. By following the points outlined in this chapter, a firm can present itself well. Beyond these points, the exporter should keep in mind that a foreign contact should be treated and served like a domestic contact. For example, the exporting company should keep customers and contacts notified of all changes, including price, personnel, address, and phone numbers.

Because of distance, a contact can "age" quickly and cease to be useful unless communication is maintained. For many companies, this means monthly or quarterly visits to customers or distributors. This level of service, although not absolutely necessary, ensures that both the company and the product maintain high visibility in the marketplace. If the exporting firm cannot afford such frequent travel, it may use fax and telephone to keep the working relationship active and up to date.

4. How to Research Your Market

To be successful, exporters must assess their markets through export research. Exporters engage in export research primarily to identify their marketing opportunities and constraints within individual foreign markets and also to identify and find prospective buyers and customers.

Market research includes all methods that a company uses to determine which foreign markets have the best potential for its products. Results of this research inform the firm of

the largest markets for its product,

the fastest growing markets,

market trends and outlook,

market conditions and practices, and

competitive firms and products.

A firm may begin to export without conducting any export market research if it receives unsolicited orders from abroad. Although this type of selling is valuable, the firm may discover even more promising markets by conducting a systematic search. A firm that opts to export indirectly by using an intermediary may wish to select markets to enter before selecting the intermediary, since many intermediaries have strengths in some markets but not in others.

A firm may research a market by using either primary or secondary data resources. In conducting primary market research, a company collects data directly from the foreign marketplace through interviews, surveys, and other direct contact with representatives and potential buyers. Primary market research has the advantage of being tailored to the company's needs and provides answers to specific questions, but the collection of such data is time-consuming and expensive.

When conducting secondary market research, a company collects data from compiled sources, such as trade statistics for a country or a product. Working with secondary sources is less expensive and helps the company focus its marketing efforts. Although secondary data sources are critical to market research, they do have limitations. The most recent statistics for some countries may be more than two years old. Product breakdowns may be too broad to be of much value to a company. Statistics on services are often unavailable. Finally, statistics may be distorted by incomplete data-gathering techniques. Yet, even with these limitations, secondary research is a valuable and relatively easy first step for a company to take. It may be the only step needed if the company decides to export indirectly through an intermediary, since the other firm may have advanced research capabilities.

Methods Of Export Research

Because of the expense of primary market research, most firms rely on secondary data sources. Secondary market research is conducted in three basic ways:

By keeping abreast of world events that influence the international marketplace, watching for announcements of specific projects, or simply visiting likely markets. For example, a thawing of political hostilities often leads to the opening of economic channels between countries.

By analyzing trade and economic statistics. Trade statistics are generally compiled by product category and by country. These statistics provide the firm with information concerning shipments of products over specified periods of time. Demographic and general economic statistics such as population size and makeup, per capita income, and production levels by industry can be important indicators of the market potential for a company's products.

By obtaining the advice of experts. There are several ways of obtaining expert advice:

Contacting experts at government agencies.

Attending seminars, workshops, and international trade shows.

Hiring an international trade and marketing consultant.

Talking with successful exporters of similar products.

Contacting trade and industry association staff.

Gathering and evaluating secondary market research can be complex and tedious. However, several publications are available that can help simplify the process.

A STEP-BY-STEP APPROACH TO MARKET RESEARCH

The exporting company may find the following approach useful.

1. Screen potential markets.

Step 1. Obtain export statistics that indicate product exports to various countries.

Step 2. Identify 5 to 10 large and fast-growing markets for the firm's product. Look at them over the past three to five years. Has market growth been consistent year to year? Did import growth occur even during periods of economic recession? If not, did growth resume with economic recovery?

Step 3. Identify some smaller but fast-emerging markets that may provide ground-floor opportunities. If the market is just beginning to open up, there may be fewer competitors than in established markets. Growth rates should be substantially higher in these countries to qualify as up-and-coming markets, given the lower starting point.

Step 4. Target three to five of the most statistically promising markets for further assessment. Consult with business associates, freight forwarders, and others to help refine targeted markets.

2. Assess targeted markets.

Step 1. Examine trends for company products as well as related products that could influence demand. Calculate overall consumption of the product and the amount accounted for by imports. Demographic information (population, age, etc.) can be obtained from World Population (Census) and Statistical Yearbook (United Nations).

Step 2. Ascertain the sources of competition, including the extent of domestic industry production and the major foreign countries the firm is competing against in each targeted market.

Step 3. Analyze factors affecting marketing and use of the product in each market, such as end user sectors, channels of distribution, cultural idiosyncrasies, and business practices.

Step 4. Identify any foreign barriers (tariff or non tariff) for the product being imported into the country

Step 5. Identify any domestic or foreign government incentives to promote exporting of the product or service.

3. Draw conclusions.

After analyzing the data, the company may conclude that its marketing resources would be applied more effectively to a few countries. In general, efforts should be directed to fewer than 10 markets if the company is new to exporting; one or two countries may be enough to start with. The company's internal resources should help determine its level of effort.

The following section describes the publications that have been mentioned and includes additional sources. Because there are many research sources, the firm may wish to seek advice from a Department of Commerce district office (see appendix III).

Sources Of Market Research

There are many domestic, foreign, and international sources of information concerning foreign markets. Several of these sources are given here. Available information ranges from simple trade statistics to in-depth market surveys.

Trade statistics indicate total exports or imports by country and by product and allow an exporter to compare the size of the market for a product among various countries.

Market surveys provide a narrative description and assessment of particular markets along with relevant statistics. The reports are often based on original research conducted in the countries studied and may include specific information on both buyers and competitors.

GENERAL INFORMATION RESOURCES

One of the best sources of information is personal interviews with private and government officials and experts. A surprisingly large number of people in both the public and private sectors are available to assist exporters interested in any aspect of international market research. Either in face-to-face interviews or by telephone, these individuals can provide a wealth of market research information.

In the private sector, sources of market research expertise include local chambers of commerce, world trade centers or clubs, and trade associations.

Sources of General Information

* Business America.

* Business America. This biweekly publication of the US Department of Commerce contains country-by-country marketing reports, incisive economic analyses, worldwide trade leads, advance notice of planned exhibitions of U.S. products worldwide, and success stories of export marketing. Annual subscriptions cost $49 (GPO:703-011-00000-4). Contact Superintendent of Documents, U.S. Government Printing Office, Washington, DC 20402; telephone 202-783-3238.

* Commerce Business Daily (CBD).

Published daily, Monday through Friday (except holidays), by the US Department of Commerce, CBD lists government procurement invitations, contract awards, subcontracting leads, sales of surplus property, and foreign business opportunities as well as certain foreign government procurements. It is available by subscription and on line (electronically). A first-class mail subscription is $260 per year or $130 for six months; second-class, $208 per year or $104 for six months (GPO:703-013-00000-7.) Contact Superintendent of Documents, U.S. Government Printing Office, Washington, DC 20402; telephone 202-783-3238.

* International Financial Statistics (IFS). Published by the International Monetary Fund, IFS presents statistics on exchange rates, money and banking, production, government finance, interest rates, and other subjects. It is available by monthly subscription for $188 yearly (yearbook, $50 alone, included in the price); single copy, $20. Contact International Financial Statistics, Publication Services, Room C100, 700 19th Street, N.W., Washington, DC 20431; telephone 202-623-7430.

* UN Statistical Yearbook. Published by the United Nations (UN), this yearbook is one of the most complete statistical reference books available. It provides international trade information on products, including information on importing countries useful in assessing import competition. The yearbook contains data for 220 countries and territories on economic and social subjects including population, agriculture, manufacturing, commodity, export-import trade, and many other areas. The latest edition available is about 900 pages and costs $100. Contact United Nations Publications, Room DC2-0853, New York, NY 10017; telephone 212-963-8302.

* World Bank Atlas. The World Bank Atlas provides demographics, gross domestic product, and average growth rates for every country. Contact World Bank Publications, 1818 H Street, N.W., Washington, DC 20433; telephone 202-473-1154.

* World Fact-book. Produced annually by the CIA, this publication provides country-by-country data on demographics, economy, communications, and defense. The cost is $23 (GPO:041-015-00169-8). Contact Superintendent of Documents, U.S. Government Printing Office, Washington, DC 20402; telephone 202-783-3238.

* Worldcasts. This eight-volume annual series presents 60,000 abstracted forecasts for products and markets for 150 countries. Forecasts are arranged by modified standard industrial classification (SIC) codes and are typically one-line entries providing short- and long-range projections for consumption, employment, production, and capacity. A product volume and a regional volume are published each quarter. The complete annual set of four product volumes and four regional volumes costs $1,300; the product set and the regional set, $900 each; single volumes, $450 each. Contact Predicasts, 11001

Cedar Avenue, Cleveland, OH 44106; telephone 800-321-6388 or
216-795-3000.

GENERAL INDUSTRY INFORMATION

* Exporters Encyclopedia.

* Exporters Encyclopedia. This extensive handbook on exporting is
updated annually and contains exhaustive, in-depth shipping and
marketing information. More than 220 world markets are covered
country by country. Topics include country profile, communications,
trade regulations, documentation, marketing data, health and safety
regulations, transportation, and business travel. The annual price is
$535. Contact Dun's Marketing Services, 3 Sylvan Way, Parsippany,
NJ 07054-3896; telephone 800-526-0651 or 201-605-6749.

*** Organization for Economic Cooperation and Development
(OECD) surveys.** These economic development surveys produced
by OECD cover each of the 24-member OECD countries
individually. Each survey presents a detailed analysis of recent
developments in market demand, production, employment, and
prices and wages. Short-term forecasts and analyses of medium-term
problems relevant to economic policies are provided. The surveys are
shipped from France. The complete set costs $180 ($203, airmail); a
single copy, $13. Contact Organization for Economic Cooperation
and Development, Publications and Information Center, 2001 L
Street, Suite 700, Washington, DC 20076; telephone 202-785-6323.

* OECD publications. OECD publishes widely on a broad range of
social and economic issues, concerns, and developments, including
reports on international market information country by country, such
as import data useful in assessing import competition. The chartered
mission of OECD is to promote within and among its 24-member
countries policies designed to support high economic growth,

employment, and standard of living and to contribute to sound economic expansion in development and in trade. For information and prices on these publications, contact Organization of Economic Cooperation and Development, Publications and Information Center, 2001 L Street, Suite 700, Washington, DC 20076; telephone 202-785-6323.

5. Export Strategy Tips and Advice

Are you interested in information regarding how to export and export strategy? There are several ways to gauge the overseas market potential of products and services. (For ease of reading, products are mentioned more than services in this guide, but much of the discussion applies to both.) One of the most important ways is to assess the product's success in domestic markets. If a company succeeds at selling in the domestic market, there is a good chance that it will also be successful in markets abroad, wherever similar needs and conditions exist.

In markets that differ significantly from the domestic market, some products may have limited potential. Those differences may be climate and environmental factors, social and cultural factors, local availability of raw materials or product alternatives, lower wage costs, lower purchasing power, the availability of foreign exchange (hard currencies like the dollar, the British pound, and the Japanese yen), government import controls, and many other factors. If a product is successful in the domestic market, one strategy for export success may be a careful analysis of why it sells here, followed by a selection of similar markets abroad. In this way, little or no product modification is required.

How to export a product? If a product is not new or unique, low-cost market research may already be available to help assess its overseas market potential. In addition, international trade statistics (available in many local libraries) can give a preliminary indication of overseas markets for a particular product by showing where similar or related products are already being sold in significant quantities.

If a product is unique or has important features that are hard to duplicate abroad, chances are good for finding an export market. For a unique product, competition may be nonexistent or very slight, while demand may be quite high.

Finally, even if domestic sales of a product are now declining, sizable export markets may exist, especially if the product once did well but is now losing market share to more technically advanced products. Countries that are less developed may not need state-of-the-art technology and may be unable to afford the most sophisticated and expensive products. Such markets may instead have a surprisingly healthy demand for products that are older or that are considered obsolete by our market standards.

Making The Export Decision

Once a company determines it has exportable products, it must still consider other factors, such as the following:

What does the company want to gain from exporting?

Is exporting consistent with other company goals?

What demands will exporting place on the company's key resources - management and personnel, production capacity, and finance -and how will these demands be met?

Are the expected benefits worth the costs, or would company resources be better used for developing new domestic business?

A more detailed list of questions is shown in below. Answers to these questions can help a company not only decide whether or not to export but also determine what methods of exporting should be initially used.

The Value Of Planning

Many companies begin export activities haphazardly, without carefully screening markets or options for market entry. While these companies may or may not have a measure of success, they may overlook better export opportunities. In the event that early export efforts are unsuccessful because of poor planning, the company may even be misled into abandoning exporting altogether. Formulating an export strategy based on good information and proper assessment increases the chances that the best options will be chosen, that resources will be used effectively, and that efforts will consequently be carried through to completion.

The purposes of the export plan are, first, to assemble facts, constraints, and goals and, second, to create an action statement that takes all of these into account. The statement includes specific objectives; it sets forth time schedules for implementation; and it marks milestones so that the degree of success can be measured and help motivate personnel.

The first draft of the export plan may be quite short and simple, but it should become more detailed and complete as the planners learn more about exporting and their company's competitive position. At least the following ten questions should ultimately be addressed:

What products are selected for export development? What modifications, if any, must be made to adapt them for overseas markets?

What countries are targeted for sales development?

In each country, what is the basic customer profile? What marketing and distribution channels should be used to reach customers?

What special challenges pertain to each market (competition, cultural differences, import controls, etc.), and what strategy will be used to address them?

How will the product's export sales price be determined?

What specific operational steps must be taken and when?

What will be the time frame for implementing each element of the plan?

What personnel and company resources will be dedicated to exporting?

What will be the cost in time and money for each element?

How will results be evaluated and used to modify the plan?

One key to developing a successful plan is the participation of all personnel who will be involved in the exporting process. All aspects of an export plan should be agreed upon by those who will ultimately execute them.

A clearly written marketing strategy offers six immediate benefits:

Because written plans display their strengths and weaknesses more readily, they are of great help in formulating and polishing an export strategy.

Written plans are not as easily forgotten, overlooked, or ignored by those charged with executing them. If deviation from the original plan occurs, it is likely to be due to a deliberate choice to do so.

Written plans are easier to communicate to others and are less likely to be misunderstood.

Written plans allocate responsibilities and provide for an evaluation of results.

Written plans can be of help in seeking financing. They indicate to lenders a serious approach to the export venture.

Written plans give management a clear understanding of what will be required and thus help to ensure a commitment to exporting. In fact, a written plan signals that the decision to export has already been made.

This last advantage is especially noteworthy. Building an international business takes time; it is usually months, sometimes even several years, before an exporting company begins to see a return on its investment of time and money. By committing to the specifics of a written plan, top management can make sure that the firm will finish what it begins and that the hopes that prompted its export efforts will be fulfilled.

The Planning Process And The Result

A crucial first step in planning is to develop broad consensus among key management on the company's goals, objectives, capabilities, and constraints. Answering the questions listed in table 1-1 is one way to start.

The first time an export plan is developed, it should be kept simple. It need be only a few pages long, since important market data and planning elements may not yet be available. The initial planning effort itself gradually generates more information and insight that can be incorporated into more sophisticated planning documents later.

From the start, the plan should be viewed and written as a management tool, not as a static document. For instance, objectives in the plan should be compared with actual results as a measure of the success of different strategies. Furthermore, the company should not hesitate to modify the plan and make it more specific as new information and experience are gained.

A detailed plan is recommended for companies that intend to export directly. Companies choosing indirect export methods may require much simpler plans. An outline of an export plan is presented in table 1-2.

Approaches To Exporting

The way a company chooses to export its products can have a significant effect on its export plan and specific marketing strategies. The basic distinction among approaches to exporting relates to a company's level of involvement in the export process. There are at least four approaches, which may be used alone or in combination:

1. Passively filling orders from domestic buyers who then export the product.

These sales are indistinguishable from other domestic sales as far as the original seller is concerned. Someone else has decided that the product in question meets foreign demand. That party takes all the risk and handles all of the exporting details, in some cases without even the awareness of the original seller. (Many companies take a stronger interest in exporting when they discover that their product is already being sold overseas.)

2. Seeking out domestic buyers who represent foreign end users or customers.

Many domestic and foreign corporations, general contractors, foreign trading companies, foreign government agencies, foreign distributors and retailers, and others purchase for export. These buyers are a large market for a wide variety of goods and services. In this case a company may know its product is being exported, but it is still the buyer who assumes the risk and handles the details of exporting.

3. Exporting indirectly through intermediaries.

With this approach, a company engages the services of an intermediary firm capable of finding foreign markets and buyers for its products. Export management companies (EMCs), export trading companies (ETCs), international trade consultants, and other intermediaries can give the exporter access to well-established expertise and trade contacts. Yet, the exporter can still retain considerable control over the process and can realize some of the other benefits of exporting, such as learning more about foreign competitors, new technologies, and other market opportunities.

4. Exporting directly.

This approach is the most ambitious and difficult, since the exporter personally handles every aspect of the exporting process from market research and planning to foreign distribution and collections. Consequently, a significant commitment of management time and attention is required to achieve good results. However, this approach may also be the best way to achieve maximum profits and long-term growth. With appropriate help and guidance from trade offices, freight forwarders, international banks, and other service groups, even small or medium-sized firms, can export directly if they are able to commit enough staff time to the effort. For those who cannot make that commitment, the services of trade consultant, or other qualified intermediary are indispensable.

Approaches number 1 and 2 represent a substantial proportion of total sales, perhaps as much as 30 percent of exports. They do not, however, involve the firm in the export process. Consequently, this guide concentrates on approaches 3 and 4. (There is no single source or special channel for identifying domestic buyers for overseas markets. In general, they may be found through the same means that buyers are found, for example, trade shows, mailing lists, industry directories, and trade associations.)

If the nature of the company's goals and resources makes an indirect method of exporting the best choice, little further planning may be needed. In such a case, the main task is to find a suitable intermediary firm that can then handle most export details. Firms that are new to exporting or are unable to commit staff and funds to more complex export activities may find indirect methods of exporting more appropriate.

An exporter may also choose to gradually increase its level of direct exporting later, after experience has been gained and sales volume appears to justify added investment.

TABLE 1-1.

Management Issues Involved in the Export Decision

Management objectives

What are the company's reasons for pursuing export markets? Are they solid objectives (e.g., increasing sales volume or developing a broader, more stable customer base) or are they frivolous (e.g., the owner wants an excuse to travel)?

How committed is top management to an export effort? Is exporting viewed as a quick fix for a slump in domestic sales? Will the company neglect its export customers if domestic sales pick up?

What are management's expectations for the export effort? How quickly does management expect export operations to become self-sustaining? What level of return on investment is expected from the export program?

Experience

With what countries has business already been conducted, or from what countries have inquiries already been received?

Which product lines are mentioned most often?

Are any domestic customers buying the product for sale or shipment overseas? If so, to what countries?

Is the trend of sales and inquiries up or down?

Who are the main domestic and foreign competitors?

What general and specific lessons have been learned from past export attempts or experiences?

Management and personnel

What in-house international expertise does the firm have (international sales experience, language capabilities, etc.)?

Who will be responsible for the export department's organization and staff?

How much senior management time (a) should be allocated and (b) could be allocated?

What organizational structure is required to ensure that export sales are adequately serviced?

Who will follow through after the planning is done?

Production capacity

How is the present capacity being used?

Will filling export orders hurt domestic sales?

What will be the cost of additional production?

Are there fluctuations in the annual work load? When? Why?

What minimum order quantity is required?

What would be required to design and package products specifically for export?

Financial capacity

What amount of capital can be committed to export production and marketing?

What level of export department operating costs can be supported?

How are the initial expenses of export efforts to be allocated?

What other new development plans are in the works that may compete with export plans?

By what date must an export effort pay for itself?

TABLE 1-2.

Sample Outline For An Export Plan

Table of Contents

Executive Summary (one or two pages maximum)

Introduction: Why This Company Should Export

Part I - Export Policy Commitment Statement

Part II - Situation/Background Analysis

Product or Service

Operations

Personnel and Export Organization

Resources of the Firm

Industry Structure, Competition, and Demand

Part III - Marketing Component

Identifying, Evaluating, and Selecting Target Markets

Product Selection and Pricing

Distribution Methods

Terms and Conditions

Internal Organization and Procedures

Sales Goals: Profit and Loss Forecasts

Part IV - Tactics: Action Steps

Primary Target Countries

Secondary Target Countries

Indirect Marketing Efforts

Part V - Export Budget

Pro Forma Financial Statements

Part VI - Implementation Schedule

Follow-up

Periodic Operational and Management Review (Measuring Results Against Plan)

Addenda: Background Data on Target Countries and Market

Basic Market Statistics: Historical and Projected

Background Facts

Competitive Environment

6. How to Finance Export Transactions

Exporters naturally want to get paid as quickly as possible, and importers usually prefer delaying payment at least until they have received and resold the goods. Because of the intense competition for export markets, being able to offer good payment terms is often necessary to make a sale. Exporters should be aware of the many financing options open to them so that they may choose the one that is most favorable for both the buyer and the seller.

An exporter may need (1) pre-shipment financing to produce or purchase the product or to provide a service or (2) post-shipment financing of the resulting account or accounts receivable, or both. The following factors are important to consider in making decisions about financing:

The need for finance export to make the sale. In some cases, favorable payment terms make a product more competitive. If the competition offers better terms and has a similar product, a sale can be lost. In other cases, the exporter may need financing to produce the goods that have been ordered or to finance other aspects of a sale, such as promotion and selling expenses, engineering modifications, and shipping costs. Various financing sources are available to exporters, depending on the specifics of the transaction and the exporter's overall financing needs.

The cost of different methods of finance export. Interest rates and fees vary. The total costs and their effect on price and profit should be well understood before a pro forma invoice is submitted to the buyer.

The length of time financing is required. Costs increase with the length of terms. Different methods of financing are available for short, medium, and long terms. However, exporters also need to be fully aware of financing limitations so that they can obtain the financing required to complete the transaction.

The risks associated with financing the transaction. The greater the risks associated with the transaction - whether they actually exist or are only perceived by the lender - the greater the costs to the exporter as well as the more difficult financing will be to obtain. Financing will also be more costly.

The creditworthiness of the buyer directly affects the probability of payment to the exporter, but it is not the only factor of concern to a potential lender. The political and economic stability of the buyer's country also can be of concern. To provide financing for either accounts receivable or the production or purchase of the product for sale, the lender may require the most secure methods of payment, a letter of credit (possibly confirmed), or export credit insurance.

If a lender is uncertain about the exporter's ability to perform, or if additional credit capacity is needed, a government guarantee program may enable the lender to provide additional financing.

The availability of the exporter's own financial resources. The company may be able to extend credit without seeking outside financing, or the company may have sufficient financial strength to establish a commercial line of credit. If neither of these alternatives is possible or desirable, other options may exist, but the exporter should fully explore the available options before issuing the pro forma invoice.

EXTENDING CREDIT TO FOREIGN BUYERS

Exporters need to weigh carefully the credit or financing they extend to foreign customers. Exporters should follow the same careful credit principles they follow for domestic customers. An important reason for controlling the credit period is the cost incurred, either through use of working capital or through interest and fees paid. If the buyer is not responsible for paying these costs, then the exporter should factor them into the selling price.

A useful guide for determining the appropriate credit period is the normal commercial terms in the exporter's industry for internationally traded products. Buyers generally expect to receive the benefits of such terms. With few exceptions, normal commercial terms range from 30 to 180 days for off-the-shelf items like consumer goods, chemicals, and other industrial raw materials, agricultural commodities, and spare parts and components. Custom-made or higher-value capital equipment, on the other hand, may warrant longer repayment periods. An allowance may have to be made for longer shipment times than are found in domestic trade, because foreign buyers are often unwilling to have the credit period start before receiving the goods.

Foreign buyers often press exporters for longer payment periods, and it is true that liberal financing is a means of enhancing export competitiveness. The exporter should recognize, however, that longer credit periods increase any risk of default for which the exporter may be liable.

Thus, the exporter must exercise judgment in balancing competitiveness against considerations of cost and safety. Also, credit terms once extended to a buyer tend to set the precedent for future sales, so the exporter should carefully consider any credit terms extended to first-time buyers.

Customers are frequently charged interest on credit periods of a year or longer but infrequently on short-term credit (up to 180 days). Most exporters absorb interest charges for short-term credit unless the customer pays after the due date.

Obtaining cash immediately is usually a high priority with exporters. One way they do so is by converting their export receivables to cash at a discount with a bank. Another way is to expand working capital resources. A third approach, suitable when the purchase involves capital goods and the repayment period extends a year or longer, is to arrange for project financing. In this case, a lender makes a loan directly to the buyer for the project and the exporter is paid immediately from the

loan proceeds while the bank waits for payment and earns interest. A fourth method, when financing is difficult to obtain for a buyer or market, is to engage in counter-trade to afford the customer an opportunity to generate earnings with which to pay for the purchase.

The options that have been mentioned normally involve the payment of interest, fees, or other costs. Some options are more feasible when the amounts are in larger denominations. Exporters should also determine whether they incur financial liability should the buyer default.

COMMERCIAL BANKS

The same type of commercial loans that finance domestic activities - including loans for working capital and revolving lines of credit - are often sought to finance export sales until payment is received. However, banks do not usually extend credit solely on the basis of an order.

A logical first step in obtaining financing is for an exporter to approach its local commercial bank. If the exporter already has a loan for domestic needs, then the lender already has experience with the exporter's ability to perform. Many exporters have very similar, if not identical, pre-shipment needs for both their international and their domestic transactions. Many lenders, therefore, would be willing to provide financing for export transactions if there were a reasonable certainty of repayment. By using letters of credit or export credit insurance, an exporter can reduce the lender's risk.

For a company that is new to exporting or is a small or medium-sized business, it is important to select a bank that is sincerely interested in serving businesses of similar type or size. If the exporter's bank lacks an international department, it will refer the exporter to a correspondent bank that has one. The exporter may want to visit the international department - of the exporter's own bank or a correspondent bank - to discuss its export plans, available banking facilities, and applicable fees.

When selecting a bank, the exporter should ask the following questions:

What are the charges for confirming a letter of credit, processing drafts, and collecting payment?

Does the bank have foreign branches or correspondent banks? Where are they located?

Can the bank provide buyer credit reports? At what cost?

What other services, such as trade leads, can it provide?

Bankers' acceptances and discounting

A time draft under an irrevocable letter of credit confirmed by a prime bank presents relatively little risk of default. Also, some banks or other lenders may be willing to buy time drafts that a credit-worthy foreign buyer has accepted or agreed to pay at a specified future date. In some cases, banks agree to accept the obligations of paying a draft, usually of a customer, for a fee; this is called a banker's acceptance.

However, to convert these instruments to cash immediately, an exporter must obtain a loan using the draft as collateral or sell the draft to an investor or a bank for a fee. When the draft is sold to an investor or bank, it is sold at a discount. The exporter receives an amount less than the face value of the draft so that when the draft is paid at its face value at the specified future date, the investor or bank receives more than it paid to the exporter. The difference between the amount paid to the exporter and the face amount paid at maturity is called a discount and represents the fees or interest (or both) the investor or bank receives for holding the draft until maturity. Some drafts are discounted by the investor or bank without recourse to the exporter in case the party that is obligated to pay the draft defaults; others may be discounted with recourse to the exporter, in which case the exporter must reimburse the investor or bank if the party obligated to pay the draft defaults. The exporter should be certain of the terms and conditions of any financing arrangement of this nature.

Project finance

Some export sales, especially sales of capital equipment, may sometimes require financing terms tailored to the buyer's cash flow and may involve payments over several years. Often the buyer obtains a loan from its own bank or arranges for other financing to enable it to pay cash to the exporter. If other project financing is required, either the exporter or the foreign buyer can initiate the proposal.

OTHER PRIVATE FINANCE EXPORT SOURCES

Factoring, forfaiting, and confirming

Factoring, forfaiting, and confirming

Factoring is the discounting of a foreign account receivable that does not involve a draft. The exporter transfers title to its foreign accounts receivable to a factoring house (an organization that specializes in the financing of accounts receivable) for cash at a discount from the face value. Although factoring is often done without recourse to the exporter, the specific arrangements should be verified by the exporter. Factoring of foreign accounts receivable is less common than factoring of domestic receivables.

Forfaiting is the selling, at a discount, of longer term accounts receivable or promissory notes of the foreign buyer. These instruments may also carry the guarantee of the foreign government. Both U.S. and European forfaiting houses, which purchase the instruments at a discount from the exporter, are active in the market. Because forfaiting may be done either with or without recourse to the exporter, the specific arrangements should be verified by the exporter.

Confirming is a financial service in which an independent company confirms an export order in the seller's country and makes payment for the goods in the currency of that country. Among the items eligible for confirmation (and thereby eligible for credit terms) are the goods themselves; inland, air, and ocean transportation costs; forwarding fees; custom brokerage fees; and duties. For the exporter, confirming means that the entire export transaction from plant to end user can be fully coordinated and paid for over time.

Export intermediaries

In addition to acting as export representatives, many export intermediaries, can help finance export sales. Some of these companies may provide short-term financing or may simply purchase the goods to be exported directly from the manufacturer, thus eliminating any risks associated with the export transaction as well as the need for financing. Some of the larger companies may make counter-trade arrangements that substitute for financing in some cases.

Buyers and suppliers as sources of financing

Foreign buyers may make down payments that reduce the need for financing from other sources. In addition, buyers may make progress payments as the goods are completed, which also reduce other financing requirements. Letters of credit that allow for progress payments upon inspection by the buyer's agent or receipt of a statement of the exporter that a certain percentage of the product has been completed are not uncommon.

In addition, suppliers may be willing to offer terms to the exporter if they are comfortable that they will receive payment. Suppliers may be willing to accept assignment of a part of the proceeds of a letter of credit or a partial transfer of a transferable letter of credit. However, some banks allow only a single transfer or assignment of a letter of credit. Therefore, the exporter should investigate the policy of the bank that will be advising or confirming the letter of credit.

7. How to Prepare Your Products for Export

In an export business, selecting and preparing a product for export requires not only product knowledge but also knowledge of the unique characteristics of each market being targeted. The market research conducted and the contacts made with foreign representatives should give the exporting company an idea of what products can be sold where. Before the sale can occur, however, the company may need to modify a particular product to satisfy buyer tastes or needs in foreign markets.

The extent to which the export business will modify products sold in export markets is a key policy issue to be addressed by management. Some exporters believe the domestic product can be exported without significant changes. Others seek to consciously develop uniform products that are acceptable in all export markets.

If the company manufactures more than one product or offers many models of a single product, it should start with the one best suited to the targeted market. Ideally, the firm chooses one or two products that fit the market without major design or engineering modifications. Doing so is possible when the company

deals with international customers with the same demographic characteristics or with the same specifications for manufactured goods,

supplies parts for domestic goods that are exported to foreign countries without modifications,

produces a unique product that is sold on the basis of its status or foreign appeal, or

produces a product that has few or no distinguishing features and that is sold almost exclusively on a commodity or price basis.

PRODUCT PREPARATION CONSIDERATIONS

What foreign needs does the product satisfy?

Should the firm modify its domestic-market product for sale abroad? Should it develop a new product for the foreign market?

What product should the firm offer abroad?

What specific features - design, color, size, packaging, brand, warranty, and so on - should the product have?

What specific services are necessary abroad at the pre-sale and postsale stages?

Are the firm's service and repair facilities adequate?

PRODUCT ADAPTATION

To enter a foreign market successfully, a company may have to modify its product to conform to government regulations, geographic and climatic conditions, buyer preferences, or standard of living. The company may also need to modify its product to facilitate shipment or to compensate for possible differences in engineering or design standards.

Foreign government product regulations are common in international trade and are expected to expand in the future. These regulations can take the form of high tariffs or of non-tariff barriers, such as regulations or product specifications. Governments impose these regulations to

protect domestic industries from foreign competition,

protect the health of their citizens,

force importers to comply with environmental controls,

ensure that importers meet local requirements for electrical or measurement systems,

restrict the flow of goods originating in or having components from certain countries, and

protect their citizens from cultural influences deemed inappropriate.

It is often necessary for a company to adapt its product to account for geographic and climatic conditions as well as for availability of resources. Factors such as topography, humidity, and energy costs can affect the performance of a product or even define its use. The cost of petroleum products along with a country's infrastructure, for example, may indicate the demand for a company's energy-consuming products.

Buyer preferences in a foreign market may also lead a manufacturer to modify its product. Local customs, such as religion or the use of leisure time, often determine whether a product will sell. The sensory impact of a product, such as taste or visual impact, may also be a critical factor. The Japanese desire for beautiful packaging, for example, has led many companies to redesign cartons and packages specifically for this market.

A country's standard of living can also determine whether a company needs to modify a product. The level of income, the level of education, and the availability of energy are all factors that help predict the acceptance of a product in a foreign market. If a country's standard of living is lower than that of the exporters', a manufacturer may find a market for less sophisticated product models that have become obsolete in his domestic market. Certain high-technology products are inappropriate in some countries not only because of their cost, but also because of their function. For example, a computerized industrial washing machine might replace workers in a country where employment is a high priority. In addition, these products may need a level of servicing that is unavailable in some countries.

Market potential must be large enough to justify the direct and indirect costs involved in product adaptation. The firm should assess the costs to be incurred and the increased revenues expected from adaptation (they may be difficult to determine). The decision to adapt a product is based in part on the degree of commitment to the specific foreign market; two firms, one with short-term goals and the other with long-term goals, may have different perspectives.

ENGINEERING AND REDESIGN

In addition to adaptations related to cultural and consumer preference, the exporter should be aware that even fundamental aspects of its products may require changing. For example, electrical standards in many foreign countries differ from the exporters'. It is not unusual to find phases, cycles, or voltages (both in home and commercial use) that would damage or impair the operating efficiency of equipment designed for use in the domestic country. These electrical standards sometimes vary even in the same country. Knowing this requirement, the manufacturer can determine whether a special motor must be substituted or arrange for a different drive ratio to achieve the desired operating revolutions per minute.

Similarly, many kinds of equipment must be engineered in the metric system for integration with other pieces of equipment or for compliance with the standards of a given country.

Since freight charges are usually assessed by weight or volume (whichever provides the greater revenue for the carrier), a company should give some consideration to shipping an item unassembled to reduce delivery costs. Shipping unassembled also facilitates movement on narrow roads or through doorways and elevators.

BRANDING, LABELING, AND PACKAGING

Consumers are concerned with both the product itself and the product's supplementary features, such as packaging, warranties, and service. Branding and labeling of products in foreign markets raise new considerations for the company:

Are international brand names important to promote and distinguish a product? Conversely, should local brands or private labels be employed to heighten local interest?

Are the colors used on labels and packages offensive or attractive to the foreign buyer? In some countries, certain colors are associated with death, national flags, or other cultural factors.

Can labels be produced in official or customary languages if required by law or practice?

Does information on product content and country of origin have to be provided?

Are weights and measures stated in the local unit?

Must each item be labeled individually?

Are local tastes and knowledge considered? A dry cereal box picturing a local athlete may not be as attractive to overseas consumers as the picture of a local sports hero.

A company may find that building international recognition for a brand is expensive. Protection for brand names varies from one country to another, and in some developing countries, barriers to the use of foreign brands or trademarks may exist. In other countries, piracy of a company's brand names and counterfeiting of its products are widespread. To protect its products and brand names, a company must comply with local laws on patents, copyrights, and trademarks. A firm may find it useful to obtain the advice of local lawyers and consultants where appropriate.

INSTALLATION

Another element of product preparation that a company should consider is the ease of installing that product overseas. If technicians or engineers are needed overseas to assist in installation, the company should minimize their time in the field if possible. To do so, the company may wish to preassemble or pretest the product before shipping.

Disassembling the product for shipment and reassembling abroad may be considered by the company. This method can save the firm shipping costs, but it may add to delay in payment if the sale is contingent on an assembled product. Even if trained personnel do not have to be sent, the company should be careful to provide all product information, such as training manuals, installation instructions, and parts lists, in the local language.

WARRANTIES

The company should include a warranty on the product, since the buyer expects a specific level of performance and a guarantee that it will be achieved. Levels of expectation for a warranty vary from country to country depending on its level of development, competitive practices, the activism of consumer groups, local standards of production quality, and other similar factors.

A company may use warranties for advertising purposes to distinguish its product from its competition. Strong warranties may be required to break into a new market, especially if the company is an unknown supplier. In some cases, warranties may be instrumental in making the sale and may be a major element of negotiation. In other cases, however, warranties similar to those in the exporters' country are not expected. By providing an unnecessary warranty, the company may raise the cost of the product higher than the competitors' costs. When considering this point, exporters should keep in mind that servicing warranties will probably be more expensive and troublesome in foreign markets. It is desirable to arrange warranty service locally with the assistance of a representative or distributor.

SERVICING

Of special concern to foreign consumers is the service the company provides for its product. Service after the sale is critical for some products; generally, the more complex the product technology, the greater the demand for pre-sale and postsale service. There is, therefore, pressure in some firms to offer simpler, more robust products overseas to reduce the need for maintenance and repairs. exporters who rely on a foreign distributor or agent to provide service backup must take steps to ensure an adequate level of service. These steps include training, periodically checking service quality, and monitoring inventories of spare parts.

8. Export Pricing, Quotations, and Terms

Proper export import pricing, complete and accurate quotations, and choice of terms of sale and payment are four critical elements in selling a product or service internationally. Of the four, export import pricing is the most problematic, even for the experienced exporter.

EXPORT IMPORT PRICING CONSIDERATIONS

At what price should the firm sell its product in the foreign market?

Does the foreign price reflect the product's quality?

Is the price competitive?

Should the firm pursue market penetration or market-skimming pricing objectives abroad?

What type of discount (trade, cash, quantity) and allowances (advertising, trade-off) should the firm offer its foreign customers?

Should prices differ with market segment?

What should the firm do about product line pricing?

What pricing options are available if the firm's costs increase or decrease? Is the demand in the foreign market elastic or inelastic?

Are the prices going to be viewed by the foreign government as reasonable or exploitative?

Do the foreign country's dumping laws pose a problem?

As in the domestic market, the price at which a product or service is sold directly determines a firm's revenues. It is essential that a firm's market research include an evaluation of all of the variables that may affect the price range for the product or service. If a firm's price is too high, the product or service will not sell. If the price is too low, export activities may not be sufficiently profitable or may create a net loss.

The traditional components for determining proper pricing are costs, market demand, and competition. These categories are the same for domestic and foreign sales and must be evaluated in view of the firm's objective in entering the foreign market. An analysis of each component from an export perspective may result in export prices that are different from domestic prices.

FOREIGN MARKET OBJECTIVES

An important aspect of a company's pricing analysis involves determining export import market objectives. Is the company attempting to penetrate a new market? Looking for long-term market growth? Looking for an outlet for surplus production or outmoded products? For example, many firms view the foreign market as a secondary market and consequently have lower expectations regarding market share and sales volume. Pricing decisions are naturally affected by this view.

Firms also may have to tailor their marketing and pricing objectives for particular foreign markets. For example, marketing objectives for sales to a developing nation where per capita income may be one tenth of per capita income in the local market are necessarily different from the objectives for Europe or Japan.

COSTS

The computation of the actual cost of producing a product and bringing it to market or providing a service is the core element in determining whether exporting is financially viable. Many new exporters calculate their export price by the cost-plus method alone. In the cost-plus method of calculation, the exporter starts with the domestic manufacturing cost and adds administration, research and development, overhead, freight forwarding, distributor margins, customs charges, and profit.

The net effect of this pricing approach may be that the export price escalates into an uncompetitive range. For a sample calculation see table 10-1 below. The table shows clearly that if an export product has the same ex-factory price as the domestic product, its final consumer price is considerably higher.

A more competitive method of pricing for market entry is what is termed marginal cost pricing. This method considers the direct, out-of-pocket expenses of producing and selling products for export as a floor beneath which prices cannot be set without incurring a loss. For example, export products may have to be modified for the export market to accommodate different sizes, electrical systems, or labels. Changes of this nature may increase costs. On the other hand, the export product may be a stripped-down version of the domestic product and therefore cost less. Or, if additional products can be produced without increasing fixed costs, the incremental cost of producing additional products for export should be lower than the earlier average production costs for the domestic market.

In addition to production costs, overhead, and research and development, other costs should be allocated to domestic and export products in proportion to the benefit derived from those expenditures. Additional costs often associated with export sales include

market research and credit checks;

business travel;

international postage, cable, and telephone rates;

translation costs;

commissions, training charges, and other costs involving foreign representatives;

consultants and freight forwarders; and

product modification and special packaging.

After the actual cost of the export product has been calculated, the exporter should formulate an approximate consumer price for the foreign market.

MARKET DEMAND

As in the domestic market, demand in the foreign market is a key to setting prices. What will the market bear for a specific product or service?

For most consumer goods, per capita income is a good gauge of a market's ability to pay. Per capita income for most of the industrialized nations is comparable to that of ours'. For the rest of the world, it is much lower. Some products may create such a strong demand - chic goods such as "Levis," for example - that even low per capita income will not affect their selling price. However, in most lower per capita income markets, simplifying the product to reduce selling price may be an answer. The firm must also keep in mind that currency valuations alter the affordability of their goods. Thus, pricing should accommodate wild fluctuations in currency, if possible. The firm should also consider who the customers will be. For example, if the firm's main customers in a developing country are expatriates or the upper class, a high price may work even though the average per capita income is low.

COMPETITION

In the domestic market, few companies are free to set prices without carefully evaluating their competitors' pricing policies. This point is also true in exporting, and it is further complicated by the need to evaluate the competition's prices in each export market the exporter intends to enter.

Where a particular foreign market is being serviced by many competitors, the exporter may have little choice but to match the going price or even go below it to establish a market share. If the exporter's product or service is new to a particular foreign market, it may actually be possible to set a higher price than is normally charged domestically.

PRICING SUMMARY

Determine the objective in the foreign market.

Compute the actual cost of the export product.

Compute the final consumer price.

Evaluate market demand and competition.

Consider modifying the product to reduce the export price.

QUOTATIONS AND PRO FORMA INVOICES

Many export transactions, particularly first-time export transactions, begin with the receipt of an inquiry from abroad, followed by a request for a quotation or a pro forma invoice.

A quotation describes the product, states a price for it, sets the time of shipment, and specifies the terms of sale and terms of payment. Since the foreign buyer may not be familiar with the product, the description of it in an overseas quotation usually must be more detailed than in a domestic quotation. The description should include the following 15 points:

Buyer's name and address.

Buyer's reference number and date of inquiry.

Listing of requested products and brief description.

Price of each item.

Gross and net shipping weight (in metric units where appropriate).

Total cubic volume and dimensions (in metric units where appropriate) packed for export.

Trade discount, if applicable.

Delivery point.

Terms of sale.

Terms of payment.

Insurance and shipping costs.

Validity period for quotation.

Total charges to be paid by customer.

Estimated shipping date to factory or port.

Estimated date of shipment arrival.

Sellers are often requested to submit a pro forma invoice with or instead of a quotation. Pro forma invoices are not for payment purposes but are essentially quotations in an invoice format. In addition to the foregoing list of items, a pro forma invoice should include a statement certifying that the pro forma invoice is true and correct and a statement describing the country of origin of the goods. Also, the invoice should be conspicuously marked "pro forma invoice." These invoices are only models that the buyer uses when applying for an import license or arranging for funds. In fact, it is good business practice to include a pro forma invoice with any international quotation, regardless of whether it has been requested. When final collection invoices are being prepared at the time of shipment, it is advisable to check with reliable source for special invoicing requirements that may prevail in the country of destination.

It is very important that price quotations state explicitly that they are subject to change without notice. If a specific price is agreed upon or guaranteed by the exporter, the precise period during which the offer remains valid should be specified.

IMPORT EXPORT TERMS OF SALE

In any export import sales agreement, it is important that a common understanding exist regarding the delivery terms. The terms in international business transactions often sound similar to those used in domestic business, but they frequently have very different meanings.

Confusion over terms of sale can result in a lost sale or a loss on a sale. For this reason, the exporter must know the terms before preparing a quotation or a pro forma invoice.

The following are a few of the more common terms used in international trade:

CIF (cost, insurance, freight) to a named overseas port of import. Under this term, the seller quotes a price for the goods (including insurance), all transportation, and miscellaneous charges to the point of debarkation from the vessel. (Typically used for ocean shipments only.)

CFR (cost and freight) to a named overseas port of import. Under this term, the seller quotes a price for the goods that includes the cost of transportation to the named point of debarkation. The cost of insurance is left to the buyer's account. (Typically used for ocean shipments only.)

CPT (carriage paid to) and CIP (carriage and insurance paid to) a named place of destination. Used in place of CFR and CIF, respectively, for shipment by modes other than water.

EXW (ex works) at a named point of origin (e.g., ex factory, ex mill, ex warehouse). Under this term, the price quoted applies only at the point of origin and the seller agrees to place the goods at the disposal of the buyer at the specified place on the date or within the period fixed. All other charges are for the account of the buyer.

FAS (free alongside ship) at a named domestic port of export. Under this term, the seller quotes a price for the goods that includes charges for delivery of the goods alongside a vessel at the port. The seller handles the cost of unloading and wharfage; loading, ocean transportation, and insurance are left to the buyer.

FCA (free carrier) to a named place. This term replaces the former "FOB named inland port" to designate the seller's responsibility for the cost of loading goods at the named shipping point. It may be used for multimodal transport, container stations, and any mode of transport, including air.

FOB (free on board) at a named port of export. The seller quotes the buyer a price that covers all costs up to and including delivery of goods aboard an overseas vessel.

The exporter should quote CIF whenever possible, because it has meaning abroad. It shows the foreign buyer the cost of getting the product to a port in or near the desired country.

If assistance is needed in figuring the CIF price, an international freight forwarder can provide help to exporting firms. The exporter should furnish the freight forwarder with a description of the product to be exported and its weight and cubic measurement when packed;

the freight forwarder can then compute the CIF price. There is usually no charge for this service.

A simple misunderstanding regarding delivery terms may prevent exporters from meeting contractual obligations or make them responsible for shipping costs they sought to avoid. It is important to understand and use delivery terms correctly.

9. Export Documentation and Shipping

When preparing for Export Documentation and Export Shipping, the exporter needs to be aware of packing, labeling, documentation, and insurance requirements. Because the goods are being shipped by unknown carriers to distant customers, the new exporter must be sure to follow all shipping requirements to help ensure that the merchandise is

packed correctly so that it arrives in good condition;

labeled correctly to ensure that the goods are handled properly and arrive on time and at the right place;

documented correctly to meet local and foreign government requirements as well as proper collection standards; and

insured against damage, loss, and pilferage and, in some cases, delay.

Because of the variety of considerations involved in the physical Export Documentation and Export Shipping process, most exporters, both new and experienced, rely on an international freight forwarder to perform these services.

FREIGHT FORWARDERS

The international freight forwarder acts as an agent for the exporter in moving cargo to the overseas destination. These agents are familiar with the import rules and regulations of foreign countries, methods of shipping, government export regulations, and the documents connected with foreign trade.

Freight forwarders can assist with an order from the start by advising the exporter of the freight costs, port charges, consular fees, cost of special documentation, and insurance costs as well as their handling fees - all of which help in preparing price quotations. Freight forwarders may also recommend the type of packing for best protecting the merchandise in transit; they can arrange to have the merchandise packed at the port or containerized. The cost for their services is a legitimate export cost that should be figured into the price charged to the customer.

When the order is ready to ship, freight forwarders should be able to review the letter of credit, commercial invoices, packing list, and so on to ensure that everything is in order. They can also reserve the necessary space on board an ocean vessel, if the exporter desires.

If the cargo arrives at the port of export and the exporter has not already done so, freight forwarders may make the necessary arrangements with customs brokers to ensure that the goods comply with customs export documentation regulations. In addition, they may have the goods delivered to the carrier in time for loading. They may also prepare the bill of lading and any special required documentation. After shipment, they forward all documents directly to the customer or to the paying bank if desired.

PACKING

In packing an item for export, the shipper should be aware of the demands that exporting puts on a package. Four problems must be kept in mind when an export shipping crate is being designed: breakage, weight, moisture, and pilferage.

Most general cargo is carried in containers, but some is still shipped as break-bulk cargo. Besides the normal handling encountered in domestic transportation, a break-bulk shipment moving by ocean freight may be loaded aboard vessels in a net or by a sling, conveyor, chute, or other method, putting added strain on the package. In the ship's hold, goods may be stacked on top of one another or come into violent contact with other goods during the voyage. Overseas, handling facilities may be less sophisticated than in your country and the cargo may be dragged, pushed, rolled, or dropped during unloading, while moving through customs, or in transit to the final destination.

Moisture is a constant problem because cargo is subject to condensation even in the hold of a ship equipped with air conditioning and a dehumidifier. The cargo may also be unloaded in the rain, and some foreign ports do not have covered storage facilities. In addition, unless the cargo is adequately protected, theft and pilferage are constant threats.

Since proper packing is essential in exporting, often the buyer specifies packing requirements. If the buyer does not so specify, be sure the goods are prepared with the following considerations in mind:

Pack in strong containers, adequately sealed and filled when possible.

To provide proper bracing in the container, regardless of size, make sure the weight is evenly distributed.

Goods should be packed in oceangoing containers, if possible, or on pallets to ensure greater ease in handling. Packages and packing filler should be made of moisture-resistant material.

To avoid pilferage, avoid mentioning contents or brand names on packages. In addition, strapping, seals, and shrink wrapping are effective means of deterring theft.

One popular method of shipment is the use of containers obtained from carriers or private leasing concerns. These containers vary in size, material, and construction and can accommodate most cargo, but they are best suited for standard package sizes and shapes. Some containers are no more than semi-truck trailers lifted off their wheels and placed on a vessel at the port of export. They are then transferred to another set of wheels at the port of import for movement to an inland destination. Refrigerated and liquid bulk containers are readily available.

Normally, air shipments require less heavy packing than ocean shipments, but they must still be adequately protected, especially if highly pilferable items are packed in domestic containers. In many instances, standard domestic packing is acceptable, especially if the product is durable and there is no concern for display packaging. In other instances, high-test (at least 250 pounds per square inch) cardboard or tri-wall construction boxes are more than adequate.

For both ocean and air shipments, freight forwarders and carriers can advise on the best packaging. Marine insurance companies are also available for consultation. It is recommended that a professional firm be hired to package for export if the exporter is not equipped for the task. This service is usually provided at a moderate cost.

Finally, because transportation costs are determined by volume and weight, special reinforced and lightweight packing materials have been devised for exporting. Care in packing goods to minimize volume and weight while giving strength may well save money while ensuring that goods are properly packed.

LABELING

Specific marking and labeling is used on export shipping cartons and containers to

meet shipping regulations,

ensure proper handling,

conceal the identity of the contents, and

help receivers identify shipments.

The overseas buyer usually specifies export marks that should appear on the cargo for easy identification by receivers. Many markings may be needed for shipment. Exporters need to put the following markings on cartons to be shipped:

Shipper's mark.

Country of origin (exporters' country).

Weight marking (in pounds and in kilograms).

Number of packages and size of cases (in inches and centimeters).

Handling marks (international pictorial symbols).

Cautionary markings, such as "This Side Up" or "Use No Hooks" (in English and in the language of the country of destination).

Port of entry.

Labels for hazardous materials (universal symbols adapted by the International Maritime Organization).

Legibility is extremely important to prevent misunderstandings and delays in shipping. Letters are generally stenciled onto packages and containers in waterproof ink. Markings should appear on three faces of the container, preferably on the top and on the two ends or the two sides. Old markings must be completely removed.

In addition to port marks, customer identification code, and indication of origin, the marks should include the package number, gross and net weights, and dimensions. If more than one package is being shipped, the total number of packages in the shipment should be included in the markings. The exporter should also include any special handling instructions on the package. It is a good idea to repeat these instructions in the language of the country of destination. Standard international shipping and handling symbols should also be used.

Exporters may find that customs regulations regarding freight labeling are strictly enforced; for example, most countries require that the country of origin be clearly labeled on each imported package. Most freight forwarders and export packing specialists can supply necessary information regarding specific regulations.

DOCUMENTATION

Exporters should seriously consider having the freight forwarder handle the formidable amount of documentation that exporting requires; freight forwarders are specialists in this process. The following documents are commonly used in exporting; which of them are actually used in each case depends on the requirements of both our government and the government of the importing country.

* **Commercial invoice.** As in a domestic transaction, the commercial invoice is a bill for the goods from the buyer to the seller. A commercial invoice should include basic information about the transaction, including a description of the goods, the address of the shipper and seller, and the delivery and payment terms. The buyer needs the invoice to prove ownership and to arrange payment. Some governments use the commercial invoice to assess customs duties.

* **Bill of lading.** Bills of lading are contracts between the owner of the goods and the carrier (as with domestic shipments). There are two types. A straight bill of lading is nonnegotiable. A negotiable or shipper's order bill of lading can be bought, sold, or traded while

goods are in transit and is used for letter-of-credit transactions. The customer usually needs the original or a copy as proof of ownership to take possession of the goods.

*** Consular invoice.** Certain nations require a consular invoice, which is used to control and identify goods. The invoice must be purchased from the consulate of the country to which the goods are being shipped and usually must be prepared in the language of that country.

*** Certificate of origin.** Certain nations require a signed statement as to the origin of the export item. Such certificates are usually obtained through a semiofficial organization such as a local chamber of commerce. A certificate may be required even though the commercial invoice contains the information.

*** Inspection certification.** Some purchasers and countries may require a certificate of inspection attesting to the specifications of the goods shipped, usually performed by a third party. Inspection certificates are often obtained from independent testing organizations.

*** Dock receipt and warehouse receipt.** These receipts are used to transfer accountability when the export item is moved by the domestic carrier to the port of embarkation and left with the international carrier for export.

*** Destination control statement.** This statement appears on the commercial invoice, ocean or air way-bill of lading, and SED to notify the carrier and all foreign parties that the item may be exported only to certain destinations.

*** Insurance certificate.** If the seller provides insurance, the insurance certificate states the type and amount of coverage. This instrument is negotiable.

*** Export license.** (when needed).

*** Export packing list.** Considerably more detailed and informative than a standard domestic packing list, an export packing list itemizes the material in each individual package and indicates the type of package: box, crate, drum, carton, and so on. It shows the individual net, legal, tare, and gross weights and measurements for each package . Package markings should be shown along with the shipper's and buyer's references. The packing list should be attached to the outside of a package in a waterproof envelope marked "packing list enclosed." The list is used by the shipper or forwarding agent to determine (1) the total shipment weight and volume and (2) whether the correct cargo is being shipped. In addition, customs officials (both local and foreign) may use the list to check the cargo.

Documentation must be precise. Slight discrepancies or omissions may prevent merchandise from being exported, result in exporting firms not getting paid, or even result in the seizure of the exporter's goods by local or foreign government customs. Collection documents are subject to precise time limits and may not be honored by a bank if out of date. Much of the documentation is routine for freight forwarders or customs brokers acting on the firm's behalf, but the exporter is ultimately responsible for the accuracy of the documentation.

The number of documents the exporter must deal with varies depending on the destination of the shipment. Because each country has different import regulations, the exporter must be careful to provide proper documentation. If the exporter does not rely on the services of a freight forwarder, there are several methods of obtaining information on foreign import restrictions:

Foreign government embassies and consulates can often provide information on import regulations.

The Air Cargo Tariff Guidebook lists country-by-country regulations affecting air shipments. Other information includes tariff rules and rates, transportation charges, air way-bill information, and special carrier regulations. Contact the Air Cargo Tariff, P.O. Box 7627, 1117 ZJ Schiphol Airport, Netherlands.

The National Council on International Trade Documentation (NCITD) provides several low-cost publications that contain information on specific documentation commonly used in international trade. NCITD provides a free listing of its publications. Contact National Council on International Trade Documentation,

350 Broadway, Suite 1200, New York, NY 10013; telephone 212-925-1400.

EXPORT IMPORT SHIPPING

The handling of transportation is similar for domestic orders and export orders. The export marks should be added to the standard information shown on a domestic bill of lading and should show the name of the exporting carrier and the latest allowed arrival date at the port of export. The exporter should also include instructions for the inland carrier to notify the international freight forwarder by telephone on arrival.

International shipments are increasingly being made on a through bill of lading under a multi-modal contract. The multi-modal transport operator (frequently one of the modal carriers) takes charge of and responsibility for the entire movement from factory to the final destination.

When determining the method of international shipping, the exporter may find it useful to consult with a freight forwarder. Since carriers are often used for large and bulky shipments, the exporter should reserve space on the carrier well before actual shipment date (this reservation is called the booking contract).

The exporter should consider the cost of shipment, delivery schedule, and accessibility to the shipped product by the foreign buyer when determining the method of international shipping. Although air carriers are more expensive, their cost may be offset by lower domestic shipping costs (because they may use a local airport instead of a coastal seaport) and quicker delivery times. These factors may give the exporter an edge over other competitors, whose service to their accounts may be less timely.

Before shipping, the firm should be sure to check with the foreign buyer about the destination of the goods. Buyers often wish the goods to be shipped to a free-trade zone or a free port where goods are exempt from import duties.

EXPORT IMPORT INSURANCE

Export shipments are usually insured against loss, damage, and delay in transit by cargo insurance. For international shipments, the carrier's liability is frequently limited by international agreements and the coverage is substantially different from domestic coverage. Arrangements for cargo insurance may be made by either the buyer or the seller, depending on the terms of sale. Exporters are advised to consult with international insurance carriers or freight forwarders for more information.

Damaging weather conditions, rough handling by carriers, and other common hazards to cargo make marine insurance important protection for exporters. If the terms of sale make the firm responsible for insurance, it should either obtain its own policy or insure cargo under a freight forwarder's policy for a fee. If the terms of sale make the foreign buyer responsible, the exporter should not assume (or even take the buyer's word) that adequate insurance has been obtained. If the buyer neglects to obtain coverage or obtains too little, damage to the cargo may cause a major financial loss to the exporter.

10. Methods of Exporting and Channels of Distribution

This article discusses Methods of Exporting and Channels of Distribution. The most common methods of export goods are indirect selling and direct selling . In indirect selling, an export intermediary normally assumes responsibility for finding overseas buyers, shipping products, and getting paid. In direct selling, the producer deals directly with a foreign buyer.

The paramount consideration in determining whether to export goods indirectly or directly is the level of resources a company is willing to devote to its international marketing effort. These are some other factors to consider when deciding whether to market indirectly or directly:

The size of the firm.

The nature of its products.

Previous export experience and expertise.

Business conditions in the selected overseas markets.

EXPORT GOODS DISTRIBUTIONS CONSIDERATIONS

Which channels of distribution should the firm use to market its products abroad?

Where should the firm produce its products and how should it distribute them in the foreign market?

What types of representatives, brokers, wholesalers, dealers, distributors, retailers, and so on should the firm use?

What are the characteristics and capabilities of the available intermediaries?

INDIRECT EXPORTING

The principal advantage of indirect marketing for a smaller company is that it provides a way to penetrate foreign markets without the complexities and risks of direct exporting. Several kinds of intermediary firms provide a range of export services. Each type of firm offers distinct advantages for the company.

Commission agents

Commission or buying agents are finders for foreign firms that want to purchase domestic products. They seek to obtain the desired items at the lowest possible price and are paid a commission by their foreign clients. In some cases, they may be foreign government agencies or quasi-governmental firms empowered to locate and purchase desired goods. Foreign government purchasing missions are one example.

Export management companies

An EMC acts as the export department for one or several producers of goods or services. It solicits and transacts business in the names of the producers it represents or in its own name for a commission, salary, or retainer plus commission. Some EMCs provide immediate payment for the producer's products by either arranging financing or directly purchasing products for resale. Typically, only larger EMCs can afford to purchase or finance exports.

EMCs usually specialize either by product or by foreign market or both. Because of their specialization, the best EMCs know their products and the markets they serve very well and usually have well-established networks of foreign distributors already in place. This immediate access to foreign markets is one of the principal reasons for using an EMC, since establishing a productive relationship with a foreign representative may be a costly and lengthy process.

One disadvantage in using an EMC is that a manufacturer may lose control over foreign sales. Most manufacturers are properly concerned that their product and company image be well maintained in foreign markets. An important way for a company to retain sufficient control in such an arrangement is to carefully select an EMC that can meet the company's needs and maintain close communication with it. For example, a company may ask for regular reports on efforts to market its products and may require approval of certain types of efforts, such as advertising programs or service arrangements. If a company wants to maintain this type of relationship with an EMC, it should negotiate points of concern before entering an agreement, since not all EMCs are willing to comply with the company's concerns.

Export trading companies

An ETC facilitates the export of domestic goods and services. Like an EMC, an ETC can either act as the export department for producers or take title to the product and export for its own account. Therefore, the terms ETC and EMC are often used interchangeably. A special kind of ETC is a group organized and operated by producers. These ETCs can be organized along multiple- or single-industry lines and can represent producers of competing products.

Export agents, merchants, or re-marketers

Export agents, merchants, or re-marketers purchase products directly from the manufacturer, packing and marking the products according to their own specifications. They then sell overseas through their contacts in their own names and assume all risks for accounts.

In transactions with export agents, merchants, or re-marketers, a firm relinquishes control over the marketing and promotion of its product, which could have an adverse effect on future sales efforts abroad. For example, the product could be under priced or incorrectly positioned in the market, or after-sales service could be neglected. On the other hand, the effort required by the manufacturer to market the product overseas is very small and may lead to sales that otherwise would take a great deal of effort to obtain.

Piggyback marketing

Piggyback marketing is an arrangement in which one manufacturer or service firm distributes a second firm's product or service. The most common piggybacking situation is when a domestic company has a contract with an overseas buyer to provide a wide range of products or services. Often, this first company does not produce all of the products it is under contract to provide, and it turns to other companies to provide the remaining products. The second company thus piggybacks its products to the international market, generally without incurring the marketing and distribution costs associated with exporting. Successful arrangements usually require that the product lines be complementary and appeal to the same customers.

DIRECT EXPORTING

The advantages of direct exporting for a company include more control over the export process, potentially higher profits, and a closer relationship to the overseas buyer and marketplace. These advantages do not come easily, however, since the company needs to devote more time, personnel, and corporate resources than are needed with indirect exporting.

When a company chooses to export directly to foreign markets, it usually makes internal organizational changes to support more complex functions. A direct exporter normally selects the markets it wishes to penetrate, chooses the best channels of distribution for each market, and then makes specific foreign business connections in order to sell its product. The rest of this chapter discusses these aspects of direct exporting in more detail.

Organizing for exporting

A company new to exporting generally treats its export sales no differently from domestic sales, using existing personnel and organizational structures. As international sales and inquiries increase, however, the company may separate the management of its exports from that of its domestic sales.

The advantages of separating international from domestic business include the centralization of specialized skills needed to deal with international markets and the benefits of a focused marketing effort that is more likely to lead to increased export sales. A possible disadvantage of such a separation is the less efficient use of corporate resources due to segmentation.

When a company separates international from domestic business, it may do so at different levels in the organization. For example, when a company first begins to export, it may create an export department with a full or part-time manager who reports to the head of domestic sales and marketing. At later stages a company may choose to increase the autonomy of the export department to the point of creating an international division that reports directly to the president.

Larger companies at advanced stages of exporting may choose to retain the international division or to organize along product or geographic lines. A company with distinct product lines may create an international department in each product division. A company with products that have common end users may organize geographically; for example, it may form a division for Europe, another for the Far East, and so on. A small company's initial needs may be satisfied by a single export manager who has responsibility for the full range of international activities. Regardless of how a company organizes for exporting, it should ensure that the organization facilitates the marketer's job. Good marketing skills can help the firm overcome the handicap of operating in an unfamiliar market. Experience has shown that a company's success in foreign markets depends less on the unique attributes of its products than on its marketing methods.

Once a company has been organized to handle exporting, the proper channel of distribution needs to be selected in each market. These channels include sales representatives, agents, distributors, retailers, and end users.

Sales representatives

The representative uses the company's product literature and samples to present the product to potential buyers. A representative usually handles many complementary lines that do not compete. The sales representative usually works on a commission basis, assumes no risk or responsibility, and is under contract for a definite period of time (renewable by mutual agreement). The contract defines territory, terms of sale, method of compensation, reasons and procedures for terminating the agreement, and other details. The sales representative may operate on either an exclusive or a nonexclusive basis.

Agents

The widely misunderstood term agent means a representative who normally has authority, perhaps even power of attorney, to make commitments on behalf of the firm he or she represents. Firms in the developed countries have stopped using the term and instead rely on the term representative, since agent can imply more than intended. Any contract should state whether the representative or agent does or does not have legal authority to obligate the firm.

Distributors

The foreign distributor is a merchant who purchases merchandise from an exporter (often at substantial discount) and resells it at a profit. The foreign distributor generally provides support and service for the product, relieving the export company of these responsibilities. The distributor usually carries an inventory of products and a sufficient supply of spare parts and maintains adequate facilities and personnel for normal servicing operations. The distributor typically carries a range of noncompetitive but complementary products. End users do not usually buy from a distributor; they buy from retailers or dealers.

The payment terms and length of association between the export company and the foreign distributor are established by contract. Some export companies prefer to begin with a relatively short trial period and then extend the contract if the relationship proves satisfactory to both parties.

Foreign retailers

A company may also sell directly to a foreign retailer, although in such transactions, products are generally limited to consumer lines. The growth of major retail chains in markets such as Europe and Japan has created new opportunities for this type of direct sale. The method relies mainly on traveling sales representatives who directly contact foreign retailers, although results may be accomplished by mailing catalogs, brochures, or other literature. The direct mail approach has the benefits of eliminating commissions, reducing traveling expenses, and reaching a broader audience. For best results, however, a firm that uses direct mail to reach foreign retailers should support it with other marketing activities.

Manufacturers with ties to major domestic retailers may also be able to use them to sell abroad. Many large retailers maintain overseas buying offices and use these offices to sell abroad when practicable.

Direct sales to end users

A business may sell its products or services directly to end users in foreign countries. These buyers can be foreign governments; institutions such as hospitals, banks, and schools; or businesses. Buyers can be identified at trade shows, through international publications, or through government contact.

The company should be aware that if a product is sold in such a direct fashion, the exporter is responsible for shipping, payment collection, and product servicing unless other arrangements are made. Unless the cost of providing these services is built into the export price, a company could end up making far less than originally intended.

Locating foreign representatives and buyers

A company that chooses to use foreign representatives may meet them during overseas business trips or at domestic or international trade shows. There are other effective methods, too, that can be employed without leaving the country. Ultimately, the exporter may need to travel abroad to identify, evaluate, and sign overseas representatives; however, a company can save time by first doing homework at home. Methods include use of banks and service organizations, and publications.

Contacting and evaluating foreign representatives

Once the company has identified a number of potential representatives or distributors in the selected market, it should write directly to each. Just as the firm is seeking information on the foreign representative, the representative is interested in corporate and product information on the export firm. The prospective representative may want more information than the company normally provides to a casual buyer. Therefore, the firm should provide full information on its history, resources, personnel, the product line, previous export activity, and all other pertinent matters. The firm may wish to include a photograph or two of plant facilities and products or possibly product samples, when practical. (Whenever the danger of piracy is significant, the exporter should guard against sending product samples that could be easily copied.)

A firm should investigate potential representatives of distributors carefully before entering into an agreement. See table 4-1 below for an extensive checklist of factors to consider in such evaluations. In brief, the firm needs to know the following points about the representative or distributor's firm:

Current status and history, including background on principal officers.

Personnel and other resources (salespeople, warehouse and service facilities, etc.).

Sales territory covered.

Current sales volume.

Typical customer profiles.

Methods of introducing new products into the sales territory.

Names and addresses of firms currently represented.

Trade and bank references.

Data on whether the exporting firm's special requirements can be met.

View of the in-country market potential for the exporting firm's products. This information is not only useful in gauging how much the representative knows about the exporter's industry, it is also valuable market research in its own right.

A company may obtain much of this information from business associates who currently work with foreign representatives. However, exporters should not hesitate to ask potential representatives or distributors detailed and specific questions; exporters have the right to explore the qualifications of those who propose to represent them overseas. Well-qualified representatives will gladly answer questions that help distinguish them from less-qualified competitors.

In addition, the company may wish to obtain at least two supporting business and credit reports to ensure that the distributor or representative is reputable. By using a second credit report from another source, the firm may gain new or more complete information. Reports are available from commercial firms.

Commercial firms and banks are good sources of credit information on overseas representatives. They can provide information directly or from their correspondent banks or branches overseas. Directories of international companies may also provide credit information on foreign firms.

If the company has the necessary information, it may wish to contact a few of the foreign firm's domestic clients to obtain an evaluation of their representative's character, reliability, efficiency, and past performance. To protect itself against possible conflicts of interest, it is also important for the firm to learn about other product lines that the foreign firm represents.

Once the company has qualified some foreign representatives, it may wish to travel to the foreign country to observe the size, condition, and location of offices and warehouses. In addition, the company should meet the sales force and try to assess its strength in the marketplace. If traveling to each distributor or representative is difficult, the company may decide to meet with them at local and worldwide trade shows.

Negotiating an agreement with a foreign representative

When the company has found a prospective representative that meets its requirements, the next step is to negotiate a foreign sales agreement.

The potential representative is interested in the company's pricing structure and profit potential. Representatives are also concerned with the terms of payment, product regulation, competitors and their market shares, the amount of support provided by the exporting firm (sales aids, promotional material, advertising, etc.), training for sales and service staff, and the company's ability to deliver on schedule.

The agreement may contain provisions that the foreign representative not have business dealings with competitive firms (this provision may cause problems in some European countries and may also cause problems under U.S. antitrust laws);

not reveal any confidential information in a way that would prove injurious, detrimental, or competitive to the exporting firm;

not enter into agreements binding to the exporting firm; and

refer all inquiries received from outside the designated sales territory to the exporting firm for action.

To ensure a conscientious sales effort from the foreign representative, the agreement should include a requirement that the foreign representative apply the utmost skill and ability to the sale of the product for the compensation named in the contract. It may be appropriate to include performance requirements such as a minimum sales volume and an expected rate of increase.

In the drafting of the agreement, special attention must be paid to safeguarding the exporter's interests in cases in which the representative proves less than satisfactory. It is vital to include an escape clause in the agreement, allowing the exporter to end the relationship safely and cleanly if the representative does not work out. Some contracts specify that either party may terminate the agreement with written notice 30, 60, or 90 days in advance. The contract may also spell out exactly what constitutes just cause for ending the agreement (e.g., failure to meet specified performance levels). Other contracts specify a certain term for the agreement (usually one year) but arrange for automatic annual renewal unless either party gives notice in writing of its intention not to renew.

In all cases, escape clauses and other provisions to safeguard the exporter may be limited by the laws of the country in which the representative is located. For this reason, the exporting firm should learn as much as it can about the legal requirements of the representative's country and obtain qualified legal counsel in preparing the contract. These are some of the legal questions to consider:

How far in advance must the representative be notified of the exporter's intention to terminate the agreement? Three months satisfy the requirements of most countries, but a verifiable means of conveyance (e.g., registered mail) may be needed to establish when the notice was served.

What is just cause for terminating a representative? Specifying causes for termination in the written contract usually strengthens the exporter's position.

Which country's laws (or which international convention) govern a contract dispute? Laws in the representative's country may forbid the representative from waiving its nation's legal jurisdiction.

What compensation is due the representative on dismissal? Depending on the length of the relationship, the added value of the market the representative has created for the exporter, and whether termination is for just cause as defined by the foreign country, the exporter may be required to compensate the representative for losses.

What must the representative give up if dismissed? The contract should specify the return of patents, trademarks, name registrations, customer records, and so on.

Should the representative be referred to as an agent? In some countries, the word agent implies power of attorney. The contract may need to specify that the representative is not a legal agent with power of attorney.

In what language should the contract be drafted? An English-language text should be the official language of the contract in most cases.

TABLE 4-1.

FACTORS TO CONSIDER WHEN CHOOSING A FOREIGN REPRESENTATIVE OR DISTRIBUTOR

The following checklist should be tailored by each company to its own needs. Key factors vary significantly with the products and countries involved.

Size of sales force

How many field sales personnel does the representative or distributor have?

What are its short- and long-range expansion plans, if any?

Would it need to expand to accommodate your account properly? If so, would it be willing to do so?

Sales record

Has its sales growth been consistent? If not, why not? Try to determine sales volume for the past five years.

What is its sales volume per outside salesperson?

What are its sales objectives for next year? How were they determined?

Territorial analysis

What territory does it now cover?

Is it consistent with the coverage you desire? If not, is it able and willing to expand?

Does it have any branch offices in the territory to be covered?

If so, are they located where your sales prospects are greatest?

Does it have any plans to open additional offices?

Product mix

How many product lines does it represent?

Are these product lines compatible with yours?

Would there be any conflict of interest?

Does it represent any other domestic firms? If so, which ones?

If necessary, would it be willing to alter its present product mix to accommodate yours?

What would be the minimum sales volume needed to justify its handling your lines? Do its sales projections reflect this minimum figure? From what you know of the territory and the prospective representative or distributor, is its projection realistic?

Facilities and equipment

Does it have adequate warehouse facilities?

What is its method of stock control?

Does it use computers? Are they compatible with yours?

What communications facilities does it have (fax, modem, telex, etc.)?

If your product requires servicing, is it equipped and qualified to do so? If not, is it willing to acquire the needed equipment and arrange for necessary training? To what extent will you have to share the training cost?

If necessary and customary, is it willing to inventory repair parts and replacement items?

Marketing policies

How is its sales staff compensated?

Does it have special incentive or motivation programs?

Does it use product managers to coordinate sales efforts for specific product lines?

How does it monitor sales performance?

How does it train its sales staff?

Would it share expenses for sales personnel to attend factory-sponsored seminars?

Customer profile

What kinds of customers is it currently contacting?

Are its interests compatible with your product line?

Who are its key accounts?

What percentage of its total gross receipts do these key accounts represent?

Principals represented

How many principals is it currently representing?

Would you be its primary supplier?

If not, what percentage of its total business would you represent? How does this percentage compare with other suppliers?

Promotional thrust

Can it help you compile market research information to be used in making forecasts?

What media does it use, if any, to promote sales?

How much of its budget is allocated to advertising? How is it distributed among various principals?

Will you be expected to contribute funds for promotional purposes? How will the amount be determined?

If it uses direct mail, how many prospects are on its mailing list?

What type of brochure does it use to describe its company and the products that it represents?

If necessary, can it translate your advertising copy?

11. International Trade Payment Methods

There are several basic Export Payment Methods - Import Payment Methods for products sold abroad. As with domestic sales, a major factor that determines the method of payment is the amount of trust in the buyer's ability and willingness to pay. For sales within our country, if the buyer has good credit, sales are usually made on open account; if not, cash in advance is required. For export sales, these same methods may be used; however, other methods are also often used in international trade. Ranked in order from most secure for the exporter to least secure, the basic methods of payment are

cash in advance,

letter of credit,

documentary collection or draft,

open account, and

other payment mechanisms, such as consignment sales.

Since getting paid in full and on time is of utmost concern to exporters, risk is a major consideration. Many factors make exporting riskier than domestic sales. However, there are also several methods of reducing risks. One of the most important factors in reducing risks is to know what risks exist. For that reason, exporters are advised to consult an international banker to determine an acceptable method of payment for each specific transaction.

CASH IN ADVANCE

Cash in advance before shipment may seem to be the most desirable method of all, since the shipper is relieved of collection problems and has immediate use of the money if a wire transfer is used. Payment by check, even before shipment, may result in a collection delay of four to six weeks and therefore frustrate the original intention of payment before shipment. On the other hand, advance payment creates cash flow problems and increases risks for the buyer. Thus, cash in advance lacks competitiveness; the buyer may refuse to pay until the merchandise is received.

DOCUMENTARY LETTERS OF CREDIT AND DRAFTS

The buyer may be concerned that the goods may not be sent if the payment is made in advance. To protect the interests of both buyer and seller, documentary letters of credit or drafts are often used. Under these two methods, documents are required to be presented before payment is made. Both letters of credit and drafts may be paid immediately, at sight, or at a later date. Drafts that are to be paid when presented for payment are called sight drafts. Drafts that are to be paid at a later date, which is often after the buyer receives the goods, are called time drafts or date drafts.

Since payment under these two methods is made on the basis of documents, all terms of sale should be clearly specified. For example, "net 30 days" should be specified as "net 30 days from acceptance" or "net 30 days from date of bill of lading" to avoid confusion and delay of payment. Likewise, the currency of payment should be specified as "US$XXX" if payment is to be made in U.S. dollars. International bankers can offer other suggestions to help.

Banks charge fees - usually a small percentage of the amount of payment - for handling letters of credit and less for handling drafts. If fees charged by both the foreign and local banks for their collection services are to be charged to the account of the buyer, this point should be explicitly stated in all quotations and on all drafts.

The exporter usually expects the buyer to pay the charges for the letter of credit, but some buyers may not accept terms that require this added cost. In such cases the exporter must either absorb the letter of credit costs or lose that potential sale.

Letters of credit

A letter of credit adds a bank's promise of paying the exporter to that of the foreign buyer when the exporter has complied with all the terms and conditions of the letter of credit. The foreign buyer applies for issuance of a letter of credit to the exporter and therefore is called the applicant; the exporter is called the beneficiary.

Payment under a documentary letter of credit is based on documents, not on the terms of sale or the condition of the goods sold. Before payment, the bank responsible for making payment verifies that all documents are exactly as required by the letter of credit. When they are not as required, a discrepancy exists, which must be cured before payment can be made. Thus, the full compliance of documents with those specified in the letter of credit is mandatory.

Often a letter of credit issued by a foreign bank is confirmed by a local bank. This means that the local bank, which is the confirming bank, adds its promise to pay to that of the foreign, or issuing, bank. Letters of credit that are not confirmed are advised through a local bank and are called advised letters of credit. Exporters may wish to confirm letters of credit issued by foreign banks not only because they are unfamiliar with the credit risk of the foreign bank but also because there may be concern about the political or economic risk associated with the country in which the bank is located. An international banker can help exporters evaluate these risks to determine what might be appropriate for each specific export transaction.

A letter of credit may be either irrevocable (that is, it cannot be changed unless both the buyer and the seller agree to make the change) or revocable (that is, either party may unilaterally make changes). A revocable letter of credit is inadvisable. A letter of credit may be at sight, which means immediate payment upon presentation of documents, or it may be a time or date letter of credit with payment to be made in the future. See the "Drafts" section of this chapter.

Any change made to a letter of credit after it has been issued is called an amendment. The fees charged by the banks involved in amending the letter of credit may be paid by either the exporter or the foreign buyer, but who is to pay which charges should be specified in the letter of credit. Since changes can be time-consuming and expensive, every effort should be made to get the letter of credit right the first time.

An exporter is usually not paid until the advising or confirming bank receives the funds from the issuing bank. To expedite the receipt of funds, wire transfers may be used. Bank practices vary, however, and the exporter may be able to receive funds by discounting the letter of credit at the bank, which involves paying a fee to the bank for this service. Exporters should consult with their international bankers about bank policy.

A Typical Letter of Credit Transaction

Here is what typically happens when payment is made by an irrevocable letter of credit confirmed by a local bank:

After the exporter and customer agree on the terms of a sale, the customer arranges for its bank to open a letter of credit. (Delays may be encountered if, for example, the buyer has insufficient funds.)

The buyer's bank prepares an irrevocable letter of credit, including all instructions to the seller concerning the shipment.

The buyer's bank sends the irrevocable letter of credit to a local bank, requesting confirmation. The exporter may request that a particular bank be the confirming bank, or the foreign bank selects one of its local correspondent banks.

The local bank prepares a letter of confirmation to forward to the exporter along with the irrevocable letter of credit.

The exporter reviews carefully all conditions in the letter of credit. The exporter's freight forwarder should be contacted to make sure that the shipping date can be met. If the exporter cannot comply with one or more of the conditions, the customer should be alerted at once.

The exporter arranges with the freight forwarder to deliver the goods to the appropriate port or airport.

When the goods are loaded, the forwarder completes the necessary documents.

The exporter (or the forwarder) presents to the local bank documents indicating full compliance.

The bank reviews the documents. If they are in order, the documents are airmailed to the buyer's bank for review and transmitted to the buyer.

The buyer (or agent) gets the documents that may be needed to claim the goods.

A draft, which may accompany the letter of credit, is paid by the exporter's bank at the time specified or may be discounted at an earlier date.

Tips on Using a Letter of Credit

When preparing quotations for prospective customers, exporters should keep in mind that banks pay only the amount specified in the letter of credit - even if higher charges for shipping, insurance, or other factors are documented.

Upon receiving a letter of credit, the exporter should carefully compare the letter's terms with the terms of the exporter's pro forma quotation. This point is extremely important, since the terms must be precisely met or the letter of credit may be invalid and the exporter may not be paid. If meeting the terms of the letter of credit is impossible or any of the information is incorrect or misspelled, the exporter should get in touch with the customer immediately and ask for an amendment to the letter of credit to correct the problem.

The exporter must provide documentation showing that the goods were shipped by the date specified in the letter of credit or the exporter may not be paid. Exporters should check with their freight forwarders to make sure that no unusual conditions may arise that would delay shipment. Similarly, documents must be presented by the date specified for the letter of credit to be paid. Exporters should verify with their international bankers that sufficient time will be available for timely presentation.

Exporters should always request that the letter of credit specify that partial shipments and transshipment will be allowed. Doing so prevents unforeseen problems at the last minute.

DRAFTS

A draft, sometimes also called a bill of exchange, is analogous to a foreign buyer's check. Like checks used in domestic commerce, drafts sometimes carry the risk that they will be dishonored.

Sight Drafts

A sight draft is used when the seller wishes to retain title to the shipment until it reaches its destination and is paid for. Before the cargo can be released, the original ocean bill of lading must be properly endorsed by the buyer and surrendered to the carrier, since it is a document that evidences title.

Air way-bills of lading, on the other hand, do not need to be presented in order for the buyer to claim the goods. Hence, there is a greater risk when a sight draft is being used with an air shipment.

In actual practice, the bill of lading or air way-bill is endorsed by the shipper and sent via the shipper's bank to the buyer's bank or to another intermediary along with a sight draft, invoices, and other supporting documents specified by either the buyer or the buyer's country (e.g., packing lists, consular invoices, insurance certificates). The bank notifies the buyer when it has received these documents; as soon as the amount of the draft is paid, the bank releases the bill of lading, enabling the buyer to obtain the shipment.

When a sight draft is being used to control the transfer of title of a shipment, some risk remains because the buyer's ability or willingness to pay may change between the time the goods are shipped and the time the drafts are presented for payment. Also, the policies of the importing country may change. If the buyer cannot or will not pay for and claim the goods, then returning or disposing of them becomes the problem of the exporter.

Exporters should also consider which foreign bank should negotiate the sight draft for payment. If the negotiating bank is also the buyer's bank, the bank may favor its customer's position, thereby putting the exporter at a disadvantage. Exporters should consult their international bankers to determine an appropriate strategy for negotiating drafts.

Time Drafts and Date Drafts

If the exporter wants to extend credit to the buyer, a time draft can be used to state that payment is due within a certain time after the buyer accepts the draft and receives the goods, for example, 30 days after acceptance. By signing and writing "accepted" on the draft, the buyer is formally obligated to pay within the stated time. When this is done the draft is called a trade acceptance and can be either kept by the exporter until maturity or sold to a bank at a discount for immediate payment.

A date draft differs slightly from a time draft in that it specifies a date on which payment is due, for example, December 1, XXXX, rather than a time period after the draft is accepted. When a sight draft or time draft is used, a buyer can delay payment by delaying acceptance of the draft. A date draft can prevent this delay in payment but still must be accepted.

When a bank accepts a draft, it becomes an obligation of the bank and a negotiable investment known as a banker's acceptance is created. A banker's acceptance can also be sold to a bank at a discount for immediate payment.

CREDIT CARDS

Many exporters of consumer and other products (generally of low value) that are sold directly to the end user accept Visa and MasterCard in payment for export sales.

International credit card transactions are typically placed by telephone or fax, methods that facilitate fraudulent transactions. Merchants should determine the validity of transactions and obtain proper authorizations.

OPEN ACCOUNT

In a foreign transaction, an open account is a convenient method of payment and may be satisfactory if the buyer is well established, has demonstrated a long and favorable payment record, or has been thoroughly checked for creditworthiness. Under open account, the exporter simply bills the customer, who is expected to pay under agreed terms at a future date. Some of the largest firms abroad make purchases only on open account.

Open account sales do pose risks, however. The absence of documents and banking channels may make legal enforcement of claims difficult to pursue. The exporter may have to pursue collection abroad, which can be difficult and costly. Also, receivables may be harder to finance, since drafts or other evidence of indebtedness are unavailable.

Before issuing a pro forma invoice to a buyer, exporters contemplating a sale on open account terms should thoroughly examine the political, economic, and commercial risks and consult with their bankers if financing will be needed for the transaction.

OTHER PAYMENT MECHANISMS

Consignment sales

Consignment sales

In international consignment sales, the same basic procedure is followed as in the local market. The material is shipped to a foreign distributor to be sold on behalf of the exporter. The exporter retains title to the goods until they are sold by the distributor. Once the goods are sold, payment is sent to the exporter. With this method, the exporter has the greatest risk and least control over the goods and may have to wait quite a while to get paid.

When this type of sale is contemplated, it may be wise to consider some form of risk insurance. In addition, it may be necessary to conduct a credit check on the foreign distributor. Furthermore, the contract should establish who is responsible for property risk insurance covering merchandise until it is sold and payment received.

Foreign currency

A buyer and a seller in different countries rarely use the same currency. Payment is usually made in either the buyer's or the seller's currency or in a mutually agreed-on currency that is foreign to both parties.

One of the uncertainties of foreign trade is the uncertainty of the future exchange rates between currencies. The relative value between the local currency and the buyer's currency may change between the time the deal is made and the time payment is received. If the exporter is not properly protected, a devaluation in the foreign currency could cause the exporter to lose money in the transaction.

One of the simplest ways for an exporter to avoid this type of risk is to quote prices and require payment in local currency. Then the burden and risk are placed on the buyer to make the currency exchange. Exporters should also be aware of problems of currency convertibility; not all currencies are freely or quickly convertible into local currency.

If the buyer asks to make payment in a foreign currency, the exporter should consult an international banker before negotiating the sales contract. Banks can offer advice on the foreign exchange risks that exist; further, some international banks can help one hedge against such a risk if necessary, by agreeing to purchase the foreign currency at a fixed price regardless of the value of the currency when the customer pays. The bank charges a fee or discount on the transaction. If this mechanism is used, the fee should be included in the price quotation.

Counter-trade and barter

International counter-trade is a trade practice whereby a supplier commits contractually, as a condition of sale, to undertake specified initiatives that compensate and benefit the other party. The resulting

linked trade fulfills financial (e.g., lack of foreign exchange), marketing, or public policy objectives of the trading parties. Not all suppliers consider counter-trade an objectionable imposition; many exporters consider counter-trade a necessary cost of doing business in markets where exports would otherwise not occur.

Simple barter is the direct exchange of goods or services between two parties; no money changes hands. Pure barter arrangements in international commerce are rare, because the parties' needs for the goods of the other seldom coincide and because valuation of the goods may pose problems. The most common form of compensatory trade practiced today involves contractually linked, parallel trade transactions each of which involves a separate financial settlement. For example, a counter-trade contract may provide that the exporter will be paid in a convertible currency as long as the exporter (or another entity designated by the exporter) agrees to export a related quantity of goods from the importing country.

Exporters can take advantage of counter-trade opportunities by trading through an intermediary with counter-trade expertise, such as an international broker, an international bank, or an export management company. Some export management companies offer specialized counter-trade services. Exporters should bear in mind that counter-trade often involves higher transaction costs and greater risks than simple export transactions.

DECREASING CREDIT RISKS THROUGH CREDIT CHECKS

Generally, it is a good idea to check a buyer's credit even if credit risk insurance or relatively safe payment methods are employed. Banks are often able to provide credit reports on foreign companies, either through their own foreign branches or through a correspondent bank.

Private credit reporting services also are available. Several services compile financial information on foreign firms (particularly larger firms) and make it available to subscribers. Reliable evaluations can also be obtained from foreign credit reporting services, many of which are listed in The Exporter's Guide to Foreign Sources for Credit Information, published by Trade Data Reports, Inc., 6 West 37th Street, New York, NY 10018.

COLLECTION PROBLEMS

In international trade, problems involving bad debts are more easily avoided than rectified after they occur. Credit checks and the other methods that have been discussed can limit the risks involved. Nonetheless, just as in a company's domestic business, exporters occasionally encounter problems with buyers who default on payments. When these problems occur in international trade, obtaining payment can be both difficult and expensive. Even when the exporter has insurance to cover commercial credit risks, a default by a buyer still requires time, effort, and cost. The exporter must exhaust all reasonable means of obtaining payment before an insurance claim is honored, and there is often a significant delay before the insurance payment is made.

The simplest (and least costly) solution to a payment problem is to contact and negotiate with the customer. With patience, understanding, and flexibility, an exporter can often resolve conflicts to the satisfaction of both sides.

This point is especially true when a simple misunderstanding or technical problem is to blame and there is no question of bad faith. Even though the exporter may be required to compromise on certain points - perhaps even on the price of the committed goods - the company may save a valuable customer and profit in the long run.

If, however, negotiations fail and the sum involved is large enough to warrant the effort, a company should obtain the assistance and advice of its bank, legal counsel, and other qualified experts. If both parties can agree to take their dispute to an arbitration agency, this step is preferable to legal action, since arbitration is often faster and less costly. The International Chamber of Commerce handles the majority of international arbitrations and is usually acceptable to foreign companies because it is not affiliated with any single country.

12. How to Make Contacts In Export

After a company has identified its most promising markets and devised strategies to enter those markets, the next step is to actually locate a buyer. If that buyer is the end user of a company's product or service, a relatively simple transaction may result. In many cases, however, exporters need an in-country presence through a representative or distributor to reach the eventual buyer. Alternatively, the firm may identify customers through attendance at trade shows, trade missions, direct mail campaigns, and advertising.

Regardless of how the exporter makes contacts and develops sales leads, the exporter faces many questions:

Specifically who are potential buyers?

What trade shows are the most effective?

Which marketing techniques are most successful?

In this chapter exporters will find the means to answer these questions. The marketing techniques described are by no means exhaustive.

BUSINESS AND SERVICE ORGANIZATION CONTACTS

Contacts made through business colleagues and associations can often prove invaluable to exporters. A colleague with firsthand experience in an international market may give a personal recommendation for an agent, distributor, or potential buyer. Conversely, the recommendation against the use of a representative for credit or reliability reasons may save the firm a number of problems. Attending export seminars and industry trade shows is an excellent method of networking with business people who have international experience. In addition, trade associations can provide a valuable source of contacts with individuals who may wish to share their experience of identifying and selling to buyers and representatives in foreign markets.

Banks can be another source of assistance in locating overseas representation. The international departments, branches, or correspondent banks of local banks may help locate reputable firms that are qualified and willing to represent exporters. In addition, freight forwarders, freight carriers, airlines, port authorities, and chambers of commerce maintain offices throughout the world. These service firms often have contacts with qualified representatives and can make recommendations to the firm. Foreign embassy and consulate commercial offices may also be able to provide directories and assistance.

PROMOTION IN PUBLICATIONS AND OTHER MEDIA

A large and varied assortment of magazines covering international markets is available to exporters through publishers. They range from specialized international magazines relating to individual industries such as construction, beverages, and textiles, to worldwide industrial magazines covering many industries. Many consumer publications produced by local-based publishers are also available. Several are produced in national-language editions (Spanish for Latin America, and so on) and also offer "regional buys" for specific export markets of the world. In addition, several business directories published in the United States and England list foreign representatives geographically or by industry specialization.

Publishers frequently supply potential exporters with helpful market information, make specific recommendations for selling in the markets they cover, help advertisers locate sales representation, and render

other services to aid international advertisers. For an extensive list of these international publications see the International Section of Business Publication Rates and Data, a book published by Standard Rate and Data Service, 5201 Old Orchard Road, Smoke, IL 60077. Another publication, The Gale Directory, contains an even more complete list of foreign periodicals, but it provides less detailed information on circulation and rates. These directories may be available at libraries.

Television, radio, and specially produced motion pictures may also be used by a business for promoting products or services, depending on the country. In areas where programs may be seen and heard in public places, television and radio promotions offer one of the few means of bringing an advertising message to great numbers of people. In many countries, particularly in Latin America, various forms of outdoor advertising (billboards, posters, electric signs, and streetcar and bus cards) are widely used to reach the mass audience.

Because of the specialized knowledge required to advertise and promote successfully in foreign markets, firms may find useful the services of an advertising agency with offices or correspondents abroad. Some agencies handle nothing but foreign advertising, and some marketing consultants specialize in the problems peculiar to selling in foreign markets.

13. After-Sales Service In Export

Three factors are critical to the success of any export sales effort: quality, price, and service. Quality and price are dealt with in other chapters. Service should be an integral part of any company's export strategy from the start. Properly handled, service can be a foundation for growth. Ignored or left to chance, it can cause an export effort to fail.

Service is the prompt delivery of the product. It is courteous sales personnel. It is a localized user manual or service manual. It is ready access to a service facility. It is knowledgeable, cost-effective maintenance, repair, or replacement. Service is location. Service is dealer support.

Service varies by the product type, the quality of the product, the price of the product, and the distribution channel employed. For export products that require no service - such as food products, some consumer goods, and commercial disposables - the issue is resolved once distribution channels, quality criteria, and return policies have been identified.

On the other hand, the characteristics of consumer durables and some consumables demand that service be available. For such products, service is a feature expected by the consumer. In fact, foreign buyers of industrial goods typically place service at the forefront of the criteria they evaluate when making a purchase decision.

All foreign markets are sophisticated, and each has its own expectations of suppliers and vendors. Manufacturers or distributors must therefore ensure that their service performance is comparable to that of the predominant competitors in the market. This level of performance is an important determinant in ensuring a reasonable competitive position, given the other factors of product quality, price, promotion, and delivery.

An exporting firm's strategy and market entry decision may dictate that it does not provide after-sale service. It may determine that its export objective is the single or multiple opportunistic entry into export markets. Although this approach may work in the short term, subsequent product offerings will be less successful as buyers recall the failure to provide expected levels of service. As a result, market development and sales expenditures may result in one-time sales. Instead of saving money by cutting back on service, the company will see lower profits (because expenses are not spread over longer production runs), ongoing sales programs, and multiple sales to developed buyers.

SERVICE DELIVERY OPTIONS

Service is an important factor in the initial export sale and ongoing success of products in foreign markets. Exporting firms have many options for the delivery of service to foreign buyers.

A high-cost option - and the most inconvenient for the foreign retail, wholesale, commercial, or industrial buyer - is for the product to be returned to the manufacturing or distribution facility in the exporters' country for service or repair. The buyer incurs a high cost and loses the use of the product for an extended period, while the seller must incur the export cost of the same product a second time to return it. Fortunately, there are practical, cost-effective alternatives to this approach.

If the selected export distribution channel is a joint venture or other partnership arrangement, the overseas partner may have a service or repair capability in the markets to be penetrated. An exporting firm's negotiations and agreements with its partner should include explicit provisions for repairs, maintenance, and warranty service. The cost of providing this service should be negotiated into the agreement.

For goods sold at retail outlets, a preferred service option is to identify and use local service facilities. Doing so requires front-end expenses to identify and train local service outlets, but such costs are more than repaid in the long run.

An excellent case study on this issue involves a foreign firm's service approach to the local market. A leading Canadian manufacturer of consumer personal care items uses local distributors and sales representatives to generate purchases by large and small retailers across the country. The products are purchased at retail by individual consumers. The Canadian firm contracted with local consumer electronic repair facilities in leading cities to provide service or replacement for its product line. Consequently, the manufacturer can include a certificate with each product listing "authorized" local warranty and service centers.

There are administrative, training, and supervisory overhead costs associated with such a warranty and service program. The benefit, however, is that the company is now perceived to be a local company that competes on equal footing with domestic manufacturers. Exporters should keep this example in mind when entering foreign markets.

Exporting a product into commercial or industrial markets may dictate a different approach. For the many companies that sell through distributors, selection of a representative to serve a region, a nation, or a market should be based not only on the distributing company's ability to sell effectively but also on its ability and willingness to service the product.

Assessing that ability to service requires that the exporter ask questions about existing service facilities; about the types, models, and age of existing service equipment; about training practices for service personnel; and about the firm's experience in servicing similar products.

If the product being exported is to be sold directly to end users, service and timely performance are critical to success. The nature of the product may require delivery of on-site service to the buyer within very specific time parameters. These are negotiable issues for which the exporter must be prepared. Such on-site service may be available from service organizations in the buyer's country; or the exporting company may have to send personnel to the site to provide service. The sales contract should anticipate a reasonable level of on-site service and should include the associated costs. Existing performance and service history can serve as a guide for estimating service and warranty requirements on export sales, and sales can be costed accordingly. This practice is accepted among small and large exporters alike.

At some level of export activity, it may become cost-effective for a company to establish its own branch or subsidiary operation in the foreign market. The branch or subsidiary may be a one-person operation or a more extensive facility staffed with sales, administration, service, and other personnel, most of whom are nationals in the market. This high-cost option enables the exporter to ensure sales and service quality, provided that personnel are trained in sales, products, and service on an ongoing basis. The benefits of this option include the control it gives to the exporter and the ability to serve multiple markets in a single region.

Manufacturers of similar or related products may find it cost-effective to consolidate service, training, and support in each export market. Service can be delivered by local-based personnel, a foreign facility under contract, or a jointly owned foreign-based service facility. Despite its cost benefits, this option raises a number of issues. Such joint activity may be interpreted as being in restraint of trade or otherwise market controlling or monopolistic. Exporters that are considering it should therefore obtain competent legal counsel when developing this joint operating arrangement.

LEGAL CONSIDERATIONS

Service is a very important part of many types of representation agreements. For better or worse, the quality of service in a country or region affects the manufacturer's reputation there.

Quality of service also affects the intellectual property rights of the manufacturer. A trademark is a mark of source, with associated quality and performance. If quality control is not maintained, the manufacturer can lose its rights to the product, because one can argue that, within that foreign market, the manufacturer has abandoned the trademark to the distributor.

It is, therefore, imperative that agreements with a representative be specific about the form of the repair or service facility, the number of people on the staff, inspection provisions, training programs, and payment of costs associated with maintaining a suitable facility. The depth or breadth of a warranty in a given country or region should be tied to the service facility to which the manufacturer has access in that market; it is important to promise only what can be delivered.

Another part of the representative agreement may detail the training the exporter will provide to its foreign representative. This detail can include frequency of training, who must be trained, where the training is provided, and which party absorbs travel and per diem costs.

NEW SALES OPPORTUNITIES AND IMPROVED CUSTOMER RELATIONS

Foreign buyers of locally-manufactured products typically have limited contact with the manufacturer or its personnel. The foreign service facility is, in fact, one of the major contact points between the exporter and the buyer. To a great extent, the manufacturer's reputation is made by the overseas service facility.

The service experience can be a positive and reinforcing sales and service encounter. It can also be an excellent sales opportunity if the service personnel are trained to take advantage of the situation. Service personnel can help the customer make life cycle decisions regarding the efficient operation of the product, how to update it for more and longer cost-effective operation, and when to replace it as the task expands or changes. Each service contact is an opportunity to educate the customer and expand the exporter's sales opportunities.

Service is also an important aspect of selling solutions and benefits rather than product features. More than one leading industrial products exporter sells its products as a "tool to do the job" rather than as a "truck" or a "cutting machine" or "software." Service capability enables customers to complete their jobs more efficiently with the exporter's "tool." Training service managers and personnel in this type of thinking vitalizes service facilities and generates new sales opportunities.

Each foreign market offers a unique opportunity for the exporter. Care and attention to the development of in-country sales and distribution capabilities is paramount. Delivery of after-sales service is critical to the near- and long-term success of the company's efforts in any market.

Senior personnel should commit to a program of regular travel to each foreign market to meet with the company's representatives, clients, and others who are important to the success of the firm in that market.

The benefits of such a program are twofold. First, executive management learns more about the foreign marketplace and the firm's capabilities. Second, the in-country representative appreciates the attention and understands the importance of the foreign market in the exporter's long-term plans. As a result, such visits help build a strong, productive relationship.

14. How to Export a Service

Export services industries span a wide variety of enterprises from hamburgers to high technology. If we take U.S. for example, The service sector accounts for about 70 percent of the U.S. GNP and 75 percent of employment. Last year, the service sector also accounted for slightly more than two-thirds of all self-employed persons.

Internationally, a similar change has taken place. World trade in export services grew in the past decade at an average rate of 5 percent a year to constitute approximately 20 percent of overall world trade today. In some countries, the share is much higher. Spain reports a 39 percent share; Austria, 36 percent. The leading exporter of services, the United States, shows services accounting for 18 percent of all merchandise and services trade and, unlike the situation with trade in goods, has had a surplus in services trade for decades.

The income generated and the jobs created through the sale of services abroad are just as important to the economy as income and jobs resulting from the production and export of goods.

TYPICAL SERVICE EXPORTS

The service sector accounts for a great share of the economy, although some services are not easily exported. It would be very difficult to export most personal services, such as the service performed by waiters in restaurants; but most business services can be exported - especially those highly innovative, specialized, or technologically advanced services that are efficiently performed domestically. The following sectors have particularly high export potential:

Construction, design, and engineering. The vast experience and technological leadership of the local construction industry, as well as special skills in operations, maintenance, and management, frequently give local firms a competitive edge in international projects. Some firms with expertise in specialized fields, such as electric power utilities, also export related construction, design, and engineering services, such as power plant design services.

Banking and financial services. financial institutions are very competitive internationally, particularly when offering account management, credit card operations, collection management, and other services they have pioneered.

Insurance services. insurers offer valuable services ranging from underwriting and risk evaluation to insurance operations and management contracts in the international marketplace.

Legal and accounting services. Firms in this field typically aid other local firms operating abroad through their international legal and accounting activities. They also use their experience to serve foreign firms in their business operations.

Computer and data services. The computer services and data industries lead the world in marketing new technologies and enjoy a competitive advantage in computer operations, data manipulation, and data transmission.

Teaching services. The vast education sector offers substantial new services for foreign purchasers, particularly in areas such as management, motivation, and the teaching of operational, managerial, and theoretical issues.

EXPORT SERVICES VERSUS PRODUCTS

There are many obvious differences between services and products. Consequently, important features differentiate exporting services from exporting products:

Services are less tangible than products, providing little in terms of samples that can be seen by the potential foreign buyer. Consequently, communicating a service offer is much more difficult than communicating a product offer. For example, brochures or catalogs explaining services often must show a proxy for the service. A construction company, for instance, can show a picture of a construction site, but a picture of the finished building communicates the actual performance of the service more effectively. Much more attention must be paid to translating the intangibility of a service into a tangible and salable offer.

The intangibility of services also makes financing more difficult. Frequently, even financial institutions with international experience are less willing to provide financial support for service exports than for product exports, because the value of services is more difficult to monitor. Customer complaints and difficulties in receiving payments can also appear more troublesome to assess.

Services are often more time dependent than products. Quite frequently, a service can be offered only at a specific time, and as time passes, the service perishes if it is not used. For example, to offer data transmission through special telephone lines may require providing an open telephone line. If this line is not heavily used, the cost of maintaining it may not be covered.

Selling services is also more personal than selling products, because it quite often requires direct involvement with the customer. This involvement demands greater cultural sensitivity when services are being provided, since a buffer of indirect communication and interaction does not exist.

Services are much more difficult to standardize than products. Service activities must frequently be tailored to the specific needs of the buyer. This need for adaptation often necessitates the service client's direct participation and cooperation in the service delivery.

Demand for certain services can derive from product exports. Many of our merchandise exports would not take place if they were not supported by service activities such as banking, insurance, and transportation. Services can be crucial in stimulating product export and are a critical factor in maintaining such exports. However, in such cases, services follow products rather than taking the lead over them.

MARKETING SERVICES ABROAD

Since service exports are often delivered in the support of product exports, a sensible approach for some beginning exporters is to follow the path of relevant product exports. For years, many large accounting and banking firms have exported by following their major multinational clients abroad and continuing to assist them in their international activities. Smaller service exporters who cooperate closely with manufacturing firms can also determine where these manufacturing firms are operating internationally and aim to provide service support for these manufacturers abroad.

For service providers whose activities are independent from products, a different strategy is needed. These individuals and firms should search for market situations abroad that are similar to the domestic market.

Many opportunities derive from understanding the process and stage of development of relevant trade activities abroad. Just as our society has undergone change, foreign societies are subject to changing economic trends. If, for example, new transportation services are opened up in a country, an expert in the area of containerization may offer services to improve the efficiency of the new system.

Leads for export services activities can also be gathered by staying informed about international projects sponsored by organizations such as the World Bank, the Caribbean Development Bank, the Inter-American Development Bank, the UN, and the World Health Organization. Very frequently, such projects are in need of service support.

15. Technology Licensing And Joint Ventures

Technology licensing is a contractual arrangement in which the licenser's patents, trademarks, service marks, copyrights, or know-how may be sold or otherwise made available to a licensee for compensation negotiated in advance between the parties. Such compensation, known as royalties, may consist of a lump sum royalty, a running royalty (royalty based on volume of production), or a combination of both. Companies frequently license their patents, trademarks, copyrights, and know-how to a foreign company that then manufactures and sells products based on the technology in a country or group of countries authorized by the licensing agreement.

A technology licensing agreement usually enables a firm to enter a foreign market quickly, yet it poses fewer financial and legal risks than owning and operating a foreign manufacturing facility or participating in an overseas joint venture. Licensing also permits firms to overcome many of the tariff and non-tariff barriers that frequently hamper the export of domestic manufactured products. For these reasons, licensing can be a particularly attractive method of exporting for small companies or companies with little international trade experience, although licensing is profitably employed by large and small firms alike. Technology licensing can also be used to acquire foreign technology (e.g., through cross-licensing agreements or grant-back clauses granting rights to improvement technology developed by a licensee).

Technology licensing is not limited to the manufacturing sector. Franchising is also an important form of technology licensing used by many service industries. In franchising, the franchisor (licenser) permits the franchisee (licensee) to employ its trademark or service mark in a contractually specified manner for the marketing of goods or services. The franchisor usually continues to support the operation of the franchisee's business by providing advertising, accounting, training, and related services and in many instances also supplies products needed by the franchisee.

As a form of exporting, technology licensing has certain potential drawbacks. The negative aspects of licensing are that (1) control over the technology is weakened because it has been transferred to an unaffiliated firm and (2) licensing usually produces fewer profits than exporting goods or services. In certain Third World countries, there also may be problems in adequately protecting the licensed technology from unauthorized use by third parties.

In considering the licensing of technology, it is important to remember that foreign licensees may attempt to use the licensed technology to manufacture products that are marketed in the exporters' market or third countries in direct competition with the licenser or its other licensees. In many instances, licensers may wish to impose territorial restrictions on their foreign licensees, depending on antitrust laws and the licensing laws of the host country. Also, patent, trademark, and copyright laws can often be used to bar unauthorized sales by foreign licensees, provided that the licenser has valid patent, trademark, or copyright protection.

As in all overseas transactions, it is important to investigate not only the prospective licensee but the licensee's country as well. The government of the host country often must approve the licensing agreement before it goes into effect. Such governments, for example, may prohibit royalty payments that exceed a certain rate or contractual provisions barring the licensee from exporting products manufactured with or embodying the licensed technology to third countries.

The prospective licenser must always take into account the host country's foreign patent, trademark, and copyright laws; exchange controls; product liability laws; possible counter-trading or barter requirements; antitrust and tax laws; and attitudes toward repatriation of royalties and dividends. The existence of a tax treaty or bilateral investment treaty between the licensers' country and the prospective host country is an important indicator of the overall commercial relationship.

Whether or not a restraint is reasonable is a fact-specific determination that is made after consideration of the availability of competing goods or technology; market shares; barriers to entry; the business justifications for and the duration of contractual restraints; valid patents, trademarks, and copyrights; and certain other factors. The U.S. Department of Justice's Antitrust Enforcement Guidelines for International Operations (1988) contains useful advice regarding the legality of various types of international transactions, including technology licensing. In those instances in which significant federal antitrust issues are presented, U.S. licensers may wish to consider applying for an export trade certificate of review from the Department of Commerce or requesting a Department of Justice business review letter.

The EC, also have strict antitrust laws that affect technology licensing. The EC has issued detailed regulations governing patent and know-how licensing. These block exemption regulations are entitled "Commission Regulation (EEC) No. 2349/84 of 23 July 1984 on the Application of Article 85(3) of the Treaty [of Rome] to Certain Categories of Patent Licensing Agreements" and "Commission Regulation (EEC) No. 556/89 of 30 November 1988 on the Application of Article 85(3) of the Treaty to Certain Categories of Know-how Licensing Agreements." These regulations should be carefully considered by anyone currently licensing or contemplating the licensing of technology to the EC.

Because of the potential complexity of international technology licensing agreements, firms should seek qualified legal advice before entering into such an agreement. In many instances licensors should also retain qualified legal counsel in the host country in order to obtain advice on applicable local laws and to receive assistance in securing the foreign government's approval of the agreement. Sound legal advice and thorough investigation of the prospective licensee and the host country increase the likelihood that the licensing agreement will be a profitable transaction and help decrease or avoid potential problems.

JOINT VENTURES

There are a number of business and legal reasons why unassisted exporting may not be the best export strategy for a company. In such cases, the firm may wish to consider a joint venture with a firm in the host country. International joint ventures are used in a wide variety of manufacturing, mining, and service industries and are frequently undertaken in conjunction with technology licensing by the firm to the joint venture.

The host country may require that a certain percentage (often 51 percent) of manufacturing or mining operations be owned by nationals of that country, thereby requiring firms to operate through joint ventures. In addition to such legal requirements, firms may find it desirable to enter into a joint venture with a foreign firm to help spread the high costs and risks frequently associated with foreign operations.

Moreover, the local partner may bring to the joint venture its knowledge of the customs and tastes of the people, an established distribution network, and valuable business and political contacts. Having local partners also decreases the foreign status of the firm and may provide some protection against discrimination or expropriation, should conditions change.

There are, of course, possible disadvantages to international joint ventures. A major potential drawback to joint ventures, especially in countries that limit foreign companies to 49 percent or less participation, is the loss of effective managerial control. A loss of effective managerial control can result in reduced profits, increased operating costs, inferior product quality, and exposure to product liability and environmental litigation and fines. Firms that wish to retain effective managerial control will find this issue an important topic in negotiations with the prospective joint venture partner and frequently the host government as well.

Like technology licensing agreements, joint ventures can raise antitrust issues in certain circumstances, particularly when the prospective joint venture partners are major existing or potential competitors in the affected national markets.

Because of the complex legal issues frequently raised by international joint venture agreements, it is very important, before entering into any such agreement, to seek legal advice from qualified counsel experienced in this aspect of international trade.

Firms contemplating international joint ventures also should consider retaining experienced counsel in the host country. Firms can find it very disadvantageous to rely upon their potential joint venture partners to negotiate host government approvals and advise them on legal issues, since their prospective partners' interests may not always coincide with their own. Qualified foreign counsel can be very helpful in obtaining government approvals and providing ongoing advice regarding the host country's patent, trademark, copyright, tax, labor, corporate, commercial, antitrust, and exchange control laws.

16. How to Get Export Advice and Tips

For companies making initial plans to export or to export in new areas, considerable export advice, export tips and assistance are available at little or no cost. It is easy, through lack of experience, to overestimate the problems involved in exporting or to get embroiled in difficulties that can be avoided. For these and other good reasons, it is important to get expert counseling and assistance from the beginning.

This chapter gives a brief overview of sources of assistance available. Other chapters in this guide give more information on the specialized services of these organizations and how to use them.

In general, however, the best place to start is the government institutions that deal with export and Commerce, they can not only provide export counseling in its own right but also direct companies toward other government and private sector export services.

Commercial banks

Good source of export advice and export tips are banks. Many banks have international banking departments with specialists familiar with specific foreign countries and various types of commodities and transactions. These large banks, located in major cities, maintain correspondent relationships with smaller banks throughout the country. Larger banks also maintain correspondent relationships with banks in most foreign countries or operate their own overseas branches, providing a direct channel to foreign customers. International banking specialists are generally well informed about export matters, even in areas that fall outside the usual limits of international banking. If they are unable to provide direct guidance or assistance, they may be able to refer inquirers to other specialists who can. Banks frequently provide consultation and guidance free of charge to their clients, since they derive income primarily from loans to the exporter and from fees for special services. Many banks also have publications available to help exporters. These materials often cover particular countries and their business practices and can be a valuable tool for initial familiarization with foreign industry. Finally, large banks frequently conduct seminars and workshops on letters of credit, documentary collections, and other banking subjects of concern to exporters.

Among the many services a commercial bank may perform for its clients are the following:

Exchange of currencies.

Assistance in financing exports.

Collection of foreign invoices, drafts, letters of credit, and other foreign receivables.

Transfer of funds to other countries.

Letters of introduction and letters of credit for travelers.

Credit information on potential representatives or buyers overseas.

Credit assistance to the exporter's foreign buyers.

Export intermediaries

Export intermediaries are of many different types, ranging from giant international companies, many foreign owned, to highly specialized, small operations. They provide a multitude of services, such as performing market research, appointing overseas distributors or commission representatives, exhibiting a client's products at international trade shows, advertising, shipping, and arranging documentation. In short, the intermediary can often take full responsibility for the export end of the business, relieving the manufacturer of all the details except filling orders.

Intermediaries may work simultaneously for a number of exporters on the basis of commissions, salary, or retainer plus commission. Some take title to the goods they handle, buying and selling in their own right. Products of a trading company's clients are often related, although the items usually are noncompetitive. One advantage of using an intermediary is that it can immediately make available marketing resources that a smaller firm would need years to develop on its own. Many export intermediaries also finance sales and extend credit, facilitating prompt payment to the exporter.

World trade centers and international trade clubs

Local or regional world trade centers and international trade clubs are composed of area business people who represent firms engaged in international trade and shipping, banks, forwarders, customs brokers, government agencies, and other service organizations involved in world trade. These organizations conduct educational programs on international business and organize promotional events to stimulate interest in world trade. Some 80 world trade centers or affiliated associations are located in major trading cities throughout the world.

By participating in a local association, a company can receive valuable and timely advice on world markets and opportunities from business people who are already knowledgeable on virtually any facet of international business. Another important advantage of membership in a local world trade club is the availability of benefits - such as services, discounts, and contacts - in affiliated clubs from foreign countries.

Chambers of commerce and trade associations

Many local chambers of commerce and major trade associations provide sophisticated and extensive services for members interested in exporting. Among these services are the following:

Conducting export seminars, workshops, and round-tables.

Providing certificates of origin.

Developing trade promotion programs, including overseas missions, mailings, and event planning.

Organizing pavilions in foreign trade shows.

Providing contacts with foreign companies and distributors.

Relaying export sales leads and other opportunities to members.

Organizing transportation routings and shipment consolidations.

Hosting visiting trade missions from other countries.

Conducting international activities at domestic trade shows.

In addition, some industry associations can supply detailed information on market demand for products in selected countries or refer members to export management companies. Most trade associations play an active role in lobbying for trade policies beneficial to their industries. Industry trade associations typically collect and maintain files on international trade news and trends affecting manufacturers. Often they publish articles and newsletters that include government research.

Chambers of commerce abroad

A valuable and reliable source of market information in any foreign country is the local chapter of our chamber of commerce. These organizations are knowledgeable about local trade opportunities, actual and potential competition, periods of maximum trade activity, and similar considerations.

Our chambers of commerce abroad usually handle inquiries from any domestic business. Detailed service, however, is ordinarily provided free of charge only for members of affiliated organizations. Some chambers have a set schedule of charges for services rendered to nonmembers.

International trade consultants and other advisers

International trade consultants can advise and assist a manufacturer on all aspects of foreign marketing. Trade consultants do not normally deal specifically with one product, although they may advise on product adaptation to a foreign market. They research domestic and foreign regulations and also assess commercial and political risk. They conduct foreign market research and establish contacts with foreign government agencies and other necessary resources, such as advertising companies, product service facilities, and local attorneys.

These consultants can locate and qualify foreign joint venture partners as well as conduct feasibility studies for the sale of manufacturing rights, the location and construction of manufacturing facilities, and the establishment of foreign branches. After sales agreements are completed, trade consultants can also ensure that follow-through is smooth and that any problems that arise are dealt with effectively. Trade consultants usually specialize by subject matter and by global area or country. For example, firms may specialize in high-technology exports to the Far East. Their consultants can advise on which agents or distributors are likely to be successful, what kinds of promotion are needed, who the competitors are, and how to deal with them. They are also knowledgeable about foreign government regulations, contract laws, and taxation. Some firms may be more specialized than others; for example, some may be thoroughly knowledgeable on legal aspects and taxation and less knowledgeable on marketing strategies.

Many large accounting firms, law firms, and specialized marketing firms provide international trade consulting services. When selecting a consulting firm, the exporter should pay particular attention to the experience and knowledge of the consultant who is in charge of its project. To find an appropriate firm, advice should be sought from other exporters and some of the other resources listed in this chapter, such as the Department of Commerce district office or local chamber of commerce.

Consultants are of greatest value to a firm that knows exactly what it wants. For this reason, and because private consultants are expensive, it pays to take full advantage of publicly funded sources of advice before hiring a consultant.

17. Glossary of Import and Export Terms

Acceptance - This term has several related meanings: (1) A time draft (or bill of exchange) that the drawee has accepted and is unconditionally obligated to pay at maturity. The draft must be presented first for acceptance - the drawee becomes the "acceptor" - then for payment. The word "accepted" and the date and place of payment must be written on the face of the draft. (2) The drawee's act in receiving a draft and thus entering into the obligation to pay its value at maturity. (3) Broadly speaking, any agreement to purchase goods under specified terms. An agreement to purchase goods at a stated price and under stated terms.

Ad valorem - According to value. See Duty.

Advance against documents - A loan made on the security of the documents covering the shipment.

Advising bank - A bank, operating in the exporter's country, that handles letters of credit for a foreign bank by notifying the export firm that the credit has been opened in its favor. The advising bank fully informs the exporter of the conditions of the letter of credit without necessarily bearing responsibility for payment.

Advisory capacity - A term indicating that a shipper's agent or representative is not empowered to make definitive decisions or adjustments without approval of the group or individual represented. Compare Without reserve.

Agent - See Foreign sales agent.

Air waybill - A bill of lading that covers both domestic and international flights transporting goods to a specified destination. This is a nonnegotiable instrument of air transport that serves as a receipt for the shipper, indicating that the carrier has accepted the goods listed and obligates itself to carry the consignment to the airport of destination according to specified conditions. Compare Inland bill of lading, Ocean bill of lading, and Through bill of lading.

Alongside - The side of a ship. Goods to be delivered "alongside" are to be placed on the dock or barge within reach of the transport ship's tackle so that they can be loaded aboard the ship.

Anti-diversion clause - See Destination control statement.

Arbitrage - The process of buying foreign exchange, stocks, bonds, and other commodities in one market and immediately selling them in another market at higher prices.

Asian dollars - U.S. dollars deposited in Asia and the Pacific Basin. Compare Eurodollars.

ATA Carnet - See Carnet.

Balance of trade - The difference between a country's total imports and exports. If exports exceed imports, a favorable balance of trade exists; if not, a trade deficit is said to exist.

Barter - Trade in which merchandise is exchanged directly for other merchandise without use of money. Barter is an important means of trade with countries using currency that is not readily convertible.

Beneficiary - The person in whose favor a letter of credit is issued or a draft is drawn.

Bill of exchange - See Draft.

Bill of lading - A document that establishes the terms of a contract between a shipper and a transportation company under which freight is to be moved between specified points for a specified charge. Usually prepared by the shipper on forms issued by the carrier, it serves as a document of title, a contract of carriage, and a receipt for goods. Also see Air waybill, Inland bill of lading, Ocean bill of lading, and Through bill of lading.

Bonded warehouse - A warehouse authorized by customs authorities for storage of goods on which payment of duties is deferred until the goods are removed.

Booking - An arrangement with a steamship company for the acceptance and carriage of freight.

Buying agent - See Purchasing agent.

Carnet - A customs document permitting the holder to carry or send merchandise temporarily into certain foreign countries (for display, demonstration, or similar purposes) without paying duties or posting bonds.

Cash against documents (CAD) - Payment for goods in which a commission house or other intermediary transfers title documents to the buyer upon payment in cash.

Cash in advance (CIA) - Payment for goods in which the price is paid in full before shipment is made. This method is usually used only for small purchases or when the goods are built to order.

Cash with order (CWO) - Payment for goods in which the buyer pays when ordering and in which the transaction is binding on both parties.

Certificate of inspection - A document certifying that merchandise (such as perishable goods) was in good condition immediately prior to its shipment.

Certificate of manufacture - A statement (often notarized) in which a producer of goods certifies that manufacture has been completed and that the goods are now at the disposal of the buyer.

Certificate of origin - A document, required by certain foreign countries for tariff purposes, certifying the country of origin of specified goods.

CFR - Cost and freight. A pricing term indicating that the cost of the goods and freight charges are included in the quoted price; the buyer arranges for and pays insurance.

Charter party - A written contract, usually on a special form, between the owner of a vessel and a "charterer" who rents use of the vessel or a part of its freight space. The contract generally includes the freight rates and the ports involved in the transportation.

CIF - Cost, insurance, freight. A pricing term indicating that the cost of the goods, insurance, and freight are included in the quoted price.

Clean bill of lading - A receipt for goods issued by a carrier that indicates that the goods were received in "apparent good order and condition," without damages or other irregularities. Compare Foul bill of lading.

Clean draft - A draft to which no documents have been attached.

Collection papers - All documents (commercial invoices, bills of lading, etc.) submitted to a buyer for the purpose of receiving payment for a shipment.

Commercial attache - The commerce expert on the diplomatic staff of his or her country's embassy or large consulate.

Commercial invoice - An itemized list of goods shipped, usually included among an exporter's collection papers.

Commission agent - See Purchasing agent.

Common carrier - An individual, partnership, or corporation that transports persons or goods for compensation.

Confirmed letter of credit - A letter of credit, issued by a foreign bank, the validity of which has been confirmed by a domestic bank. An exporter whose payment terms are a confirmed letter of credit is assured of payment by the domestic bank even if the foreign buyer or the foreign bank defaults. See Letter of credit.

Consignment - Delivery of merchandise from an exporter (the consignor) to an agent (the consignee) under agreement that the agent sell the merchandise for the account of the exporter. The consignor retains title to the goods until the consignee has sold them. The consignee sells the goods for commission and remits the net proceeds to the consignor.

Consular declaration - A formal statement, made to the consul of a foreign country, describing goods to be shipped.

Consular invoice - A document, required by some foreign countries, describing a shipment of goods and showing information such as the consignor, consignee, and value of the shipment. Certified by a consular official of the foreign country, it is used by the country's customs officials to verify the value, quantity, and nature of the shipment.

Convertible currency - A currency that can be bought and sold for other currencies at will.

Correspondent bank - A bank that, in its own country, handles the business of a foreign bank.

Counter-trade - The sale of goods or services that are paid for in whole or in part by the transfer of goods or services from a foreign country.

Countervailing duty - A duty imposed to counter unfairly subsidized products.

CPT (carriage paid to) and CIP (carriage and insurance paid to) - Pricing terms indicating that carriage, or carriage and insurance, are paid to the named place of destination. They apply in place of CFR and CIF, respectively, for shipment by modes other than water.

Credit risk insurance - Insurance designed to cover risks of nonpayment for delivered goods. Compare Marine insurance.

Customhouse broker - An individual or firm licensed to enter and clear goods through customs.

Customs - The authorities designated to collect duties levied by a country on imports and exports. The term also applies to the procedures involved in such collection.

Date draft - A draft that matures in a specified number of days after the date it is issued, without regard to the date of acceptance. See Draft, Sight draft, and Time draft.

Deferred payment credit - Type of letter of credit providing for payment some time after presentation of shipping documents by exporter.

Demand draft - See Sight draft.

Devaluation - The official lowering of the value of one country's currency in terms of one or more foreign currencies. For example, if the U.S. dollar is devalued in relation to the French franc, one dollar will "buy" fewer francs than before.

DISC - Domestic international sales corporation. Discrepancy - Letter of credit - When documents presented do not conform to the letter of credit it is referred to as a discrepancy.

Dispatch - An amount paid by a vessel's operator to a charterer if loading or unloading is completed in less time than stipulated in the charter party.

Distributor - A foreign agent who sells for a supplier directly and maintains an inventory of the supplier's products.

Dock receipt - A receipt issued by an ocean carrier to acknowledge receipt of a shipment at the carrier's dock or warehouse facilities. Also see Warehouse receipt.

Documentary draft - A draft to which documents are attached.

Documents against acceptance (D/A) - Instructions given by a shipper to a bank indicating that documents transferring title to goods should be delivered to the buyer (or drawee) only upon the buyer's acceptance of the attached draft.

Draft (or Bill of exchange) - An unconditional order in writing from one person (the drawer) to another (the drawee), directing the drawee to pay a specified amount to a named drawer at a fixed or determinable future date. See Date draft, Sight draft, Time draft.

Drawback - Articles manufactured or produced in the United States with the use of imported components or raw materials and later exported are entitled to a refund of up to 99 percent of the duty charged on the imported components. The refund of duty is known as a drawback.

Drawee - The individual or firm on whom a draft is drawn and who owes the stated amount. Compare Drawer. Also see Draft.

Drawer - The individual or firm that issues or signs a draft and thus stands to receive payment of the stated amount from the drawee. Compare Drawee. Also see Draft.

Dumping - Selling merchandise in another country at a price below the price at which the same merchandise is sold in the home market or selling such merchandise below the costs incurred in production and shipment.

Duty - A tax imposed on imports by the customs authority of a country. Duties are generally based on the value of the goods (ad valorem duties), some other factor such as weight or quantity (specific duties), or a combination of value and other factors (compound duties).

EMC - See Export management company.

ETC - See Export trading company.

Eurodollars - U.S. dollars placed on deposit in banks outside the United States; usually refers to deposits in Europe.

Ex - From. When used in pricing terms such as "ex factory" or "ex dock," it signifies that the price quoted applies only at the point of origin (in the two examples, at the seller's factory or a dock at the import point). In practice, this kind of quotation indicates that the seller agrees to place the goods at the disposal of the buyer at the specified place within a fixed period of time.

Exchange permit - A government permit sometimes required by the importer's government to enable the import firm to convert its own country's currency into foreign currency with which to pay a seller in another country.

Exchange rate - The price of one currency in terms of another, that is, the number of units of one currency that may be exchanged for one unit of another currency.

Eximbank - Export-Import Bank of the United States.

Export broker - An individual or firm that brings together buyers and sellers for a fee but does not take part in actual sales transactions.

Export commission house - An organization which, for a commission, acts as a purchasing agent for a foreign buyer.

Export declaration - See Shipper's export declaration.

Export license - A government document that permits the licensee to export designated goods to certain destinations. See General export license and Individually validated export license.

Export management company - A private firm that serves as the export department for several producers of goods or services, either by taking title or by soliciting and transacting export business on behalf of its clients in return for a commission, salary, or retainer plus commission.

Export trading company - A firm similar or identical to an export management company.

FAS - Free alongside ship. A pricing term indicating that the quoted price includes the cost of delivering the goods alongside a designated vessel.

FCA - "Free carrier" to named place. Replaces the former term "FOB named inland port" to designate the seller's responsibility for the cost of loading goods at the named shipping point. May be used for multi-modal transport, container stations, and any mode of transport, including air.

FCIA - Foreign Credit Insurance Association.

FI - Free in. A pricing term indicating that the charterer of a vessel is responsible for the cost of loading and unloading goods from the vessel.

Floating policy - See Open policy.

FO - Free out. A pricing term indicating that the charterer of a vessel is responsible for the cost of loading goods from the vessel.

FOB - "Free on board" at named port of export. A pricing term indicating that the quoted price covers all expenses up to and including delivery of goods upon an overseas vessel provided by or for the buyer.

Force majeure - The title of a standard clause in marine contracts exempting the parties for non-fulfillment of their obligations as a result of conditions beyond their control, such as earthquakes, floods, or war.

Foreign exchange - The currency or credit instruments of a foreign country. Also, transactions involving purchase or sale of currencies.

Foreign freight forwarder - See Freight forwarder.

Foreign sales agent - An individual or firm that serves as the foreign representative of a domestic supplier and seeks sales abroad for the supplier.

Foreign trade zone - See Free-trade zone.

Foul bill of lading - A receipt for goods issued by a carrier with an indication that the goods were damaged when received. Compare Clean bill of lading.

Free port - An area such as a port city into which merchandise may legally be moved without payment of duties.

Free-trade zone - A port designated by the government of a country for duty-free entry of any non-prohibited goods. Merchandise may be stored, displayed, used for manufacturing, etc., within the zone and reexported without duties being paid. Duties are imposed on the merchandise (or items manufactured from the merchandise) only when the goods pass from the zone into an area of the country subject to the customs authority.

Freight forwarder - An independent business that handles export shipments for compensation. (A freight forwarder is among the best sources of information and assistance on export regulations and documentation, shipping methods, and foreign import regulations.)

GATT - General Agreement on Tariffs and Trade. A multilateral treaty intended to help reduce trade barriers between signatory countries and to promote trade through tariff concessions.

General export license - Any of various export licenses covering export commodities for which Individually validated export licenses are not required. No formal application or written authorization is needed to ship exports under a general export license.

Gross weight - The full weight of a shipment, including goods and packaging. Compare Tare weight.

Import license - A document required and issued by some national governments authorizing the importation of goods into their individual countries.

Individually validated export license - A required document issued by the U.S. Government authorizing the export of specific commodities. This license is for a specific transaction or time period in which the exporting is to take place. Compare General export license.

Inland bill of lading - A bill of lading used in transporting goods overland to the exporter's international carrier. Although a through bill of lading can sometimes be used, it is usually necessary to prepare both an inland bill of lading and an ocean bill of lading for export shipments. Compare Air waybill, Ocean bill of lading, and Through bill of lading.

International freight forwarder - See Freight forwarder.

Irrevocable letter of credit - A letter of credit in which the specified payment is guaranteed by the bank if all terms and conditions are met by the drawee. Compare Revocable letter of credit.

Letter of credit (L/C) - A document, issued by a bank per instructions by a buyer of goods, authorizing the seller to draw a specified sum of money under specified terms, usually the receipt by the bank of certain documents within a given time.

Licensing - A business arrangement in which the manufacturer of a product (or a firm with proprietary rights over certain technology, trademarks, etc.) grants permission to some other group or individual to manufacture that product (or make use of that proprietary material) in return for specified royalties or other payment.

Manifest - See Ship's manifest.

Marine insurance - Insurance that compensates the owners of goods transported overseas in the event of loss that cannot be legally recovered from the carrier. Also covers air shipments. Compare Credit risk insurance.

Marking (or marks) - Letters, numbers, and other symbols placed on cargo packages to facilitate identification.

Ocean bill of lading - A bill of lading (B/L) indicating that the exporter consigns a shipment to an international carrier for transportation to a specified foreign market. Unlike an inland B/L, the ocean B/L also serves as a collection document. If it is a "straight" B/L, the foreign buyer can obtain the shipment from the carrier by simply showing proof of identity. If a "negotiable" B/L is used, the buyer must first pay for the goods, post a bond, or meet other conditions agreeable to the seller. Compare Air waybill, Inland bill of lading, and Through bill of lading.

On board bill of lading - A bill of lading in which a carrier certifies that goods have been placed on board a certain vessel.

Open account - A trade arrangement in which goods are shipped to a foreign buyer without guarantee of payment. The obvious risk this method poses to the supplier makes it essential that the buyer's integrity be unquestionable.

Open insurance policy - A marine insurance policy that applies to all shipments made by an exporter over a period of time rather than to one shipment only.

Order bill of lading - A negotiable bill of lading made out to the order of the shipper.

Packing list - A list showing the number and kinds of items being shipped, as well as other information needed for transportation purposes.

Parcel post receipt - The postal authorities' signed acknowledgment of delivery to receiver of a shipment made by parcel post.

PEFCO - Private Export Funding Corporation. A corporation that lends to foreign buyers to finance exports from the United States.

Perils of the sea - A marine insurance term used to designate heavy weather, stranding, lightning, collision, and sea water damage.

Phytosanitary inspection certificate - A certificate, issued by the U.S. Department of Agriculture to satisfy import regulations for foreign countries, indicating that a U.S. shipment has been inspected and is free from harmful pests and plant diseases.

Political risk - In export financing, the risk of loss due to such causes as currency inconvertibility, government action preventing entry of goods, expropriation or confiscation, and war.

Pro forma invoice - An invoice provided by a supplier prior to the shipment of merchandise, informing the buyer of the kinds and quantities of goods to be sent, their value, and important specifications (weight, size, etc.).

Purchasing agent - An agent who purchases goods in his or her own country on behalf of foreign importers such as government agencies and large private concerns.

Quota - The quantity of goods of a specific kind that a country permits to be imported without restriction or imposition of additional duties.

Quotation - An offer to sell goods at a stated price and under specified conditions.

Remitting bank - The bank that sends the draft to the overseas bank for collection.

Representative - See Foreign sales agent.

Revocable letter of credit - A letter of credit that can be canceled or altered by the drawee (buyer) after it has been issued by the drawee's bank. Compare Irrevocable letter of credit.

Shipper's export declaration - A form required for all shipments by the U.S. Treasury Department and prepared by a shipper, indicating the value, weight, destination, and other basic information about an export shipment.

Ship's manifest - An instrument in writing, signed by the captain of a ship, that lists the individual shipments constituting the ship's cargo.

Sight draft (S/D) - A draft that is payable upon presentation to the drawee. Compare Date draft and Time draft.

Spot exchange - The purchase or sale of foreign exchange for immediate delivery.

Standard industrial classification (SIC) - A standard numerical code system used to classify products and services.

Standard international trade classification (SITC) - A standard numerical code system developed by the United Nations to classify commodities used in international trade.

Steamship conference - A group of steamship operators that operate under mutually agreed-upon freight rates.

Straight bill of lading - A nonnegotiable bill of lading in which the goods are consigned directly to a named consignee.

Tare weight - The weight of a container and packing materials without the weight of the goods it contains. Compare Gross weight.

Tenor (of a draft) - Designation of a payment as being due at sight, a given number of days after sight, or a given number of days after date.

Through bill of lading - A single bill of lading converting both the domestic and international carriage of an export shipment. An air waybill, for instance, is essentially a through bill of lading used for air shipments. Ocean shipments, on the other hand, usually require two separate documents - an inland bill of lading for domestic carriage and an ocean bill of lading for international carriage. Through bills of lading are insufficient for ocean shipments. Compare Air waybill, Inland bill of lading, and Ocean bill of lading.

Time draft - A draft that matures either a certain number of days after acceptance or a certain number of days after the date of the draft. Compare Date draft and Sight draft (see chapter 13).

Tramp steamer - A ship not operating on regular routes or schedules.

Transaction statement - A document that delineates the terms and conditions agreed upon between the importer and exporter.

Trust receipt - Release of merchandise by a bank to a buyer in which the bank retains title to the merchandise. The buyer, who obtains the goods for manufacturing or sales purposes, is obligated to maintain the goods (or the proceeds from their sale) distinct from the remainder of his or her assets and to hold them ready for repossession by the bank.

Warehouse receipt - A receipt issued by a warehouse listing goods received for storage.

Wharfage - A charge assessed by a pier or dock owner for handling incoming or outgoing cargo.

Without reserve - A term indicating that a shipper's agent or representative is empowered to make definitive decisions and adjustments abroad without approval of the group or individual represented. Compare Advisory capacity.

18. Business Travel Tips

Business world travel abroad can locate and cultivate new customers and improve relationships and communication with current foreign representatives and associates. As in domestic business, there is nothing like a face-to-face meeting with a client or customer.

The following suggestions can help companies prepare for a business world travel trip. By keeping in mind that even little things (such as forgetting to check foreign holiday schedules or neglecting to arrange for translator services) can cost time, opportunity, and money, a firm can get maximum value from its time spent abroad.

PLANNING THE ITINERARY

A well-planned itinerary enables a traveler to make the best possible use of time abroad. Although travel time is expensive, care must be taken not to overload the schedule. Two or three definite appointments, confirmed well in advance and spaced comfortably throughout one day, are more productive and enjoyable than a crowded agenda that forces the business person to rush from one meeting to the next before business is really concluded. If possible, an extra rest day to deal with jet lag should be planned before scheduled business appointments. The following travel tips should be kept in mind:

The travel plans should reflect what the company hopes to accomplish. The traveler should give some thought to the trip's goals and their relative priorities.

The traveler should accomplish as much as possible before the trip begins by obtaining names of possible contacts, arranging appointments, checking transportation schedules, and so on. The most important meetings should be confirmed before the traveler leaves the country.

As a general rule, the business person should keep the schedule flexible enough to allow for both unexpected problems (such as transportation delays) and unexpected opportunities. For instance, accepting an unscheduled luncheon invitation from a prospective client should not make it necessary to miss the next scheduled meeting.

The traveler should check the normal work days and business hours in the countries to be visited. In many Middle Eastern regions, for instance, the work week typically runs from Saturday to Thursday. In many countries, lunch hours of two to four hours are customary.

Along the same lines, take foreign holidays into account.

The business person should be aware that travel from one country to another may be restricted. For example, a passport containing an Israeli visa may disallow the traveler from entering certain countries in the Middle East.

OTHER PREPARATIONS

Travel agents can frequently arrange for transportation and hotel reservations quickly and efficiently. They can also help plan the itinerary, obtain the best travel rates, explain which countries require visas, advise on hotel rates and locations, and provide other valuable services. Since travel agents' fees are paid by the hotels, airlines, and other carriers, this assistance and expertise may cost nothing.

The traveler should obtain the necessary travel documents two to three months before departure, especially if visas are needed. A travel agent can help make the arrangements. A valid passport is required for all travel outside the country. If traveling on an old passport, you should make sure that it remains valid for the entire duration of the trip.

Visas, which are required by many countries, are provided for a small fee by the foreign country's embassy or consulate. To obtain a visa, the traveler must have a current passport. In addition, many countries require a recent photo. The traveler should allow several weeks to obtain visas, especially if traveling to developing nations. Some countries that do not require visas for tourist travel do require them for business travel. Visa requirements may change from time to time.

Requirements for vaccinations differ from country to country. A travel agent or airline can advise the traveler on various requirements.

In some cases, vaccinations against typhus, typhoid, and other diseases are advisable even though they are not required.

BUSINESS PREPARATIONS FOR INTERNATIONAL TRAVEL

Before leaving the country, the traveler should prepare to deal with language differences by learning whether individuals to be met are comfortable speaking English. If not, plans should be made for an interpreter. Business language is generally more technical than the conversational speech with which many travelers are familiar; mistakes can be costly.

In some countries, exchanging business cards at any first meeting is considered a basic part of good business manners. As a matter of courtesy, it is best to carry business cards printed both in English and in the language of the country being visited. Some international airlines arrange this service.

The following travel checklist covers a number of considerations that apply equally to business travelers and vacationers. A travel agent or various travel publications can help take these considerations into account:

Seasonal weather conditions in the countries being visited.

Health care (e.g., what to eat abroad, special medical problems, and prescription drugs)

Electrical current (a transformer or plug adapter may be needed to use electrical appliances).

Money (e.g., exchanging currency and using credit cards and travelers' checks).

Transportation. (Infrastructure, vehicle and operations.)

Communication- (International phone cards, free calling option, roaming facilities for business or family reasons)

Cultural differences.

Tipping (who is tipped and how much is appropriate).

Customs regulations on what can be brought home.

CARNETS

Foreign customs regulations vary widely from place to place, and the traveler is wise to learn in advance the regulations that apply to each

country to be visited. If allowances for cigarettes, liquor, currency, and certain other items are not taken into account, they can be impounded at national borders. Business travelers who plan to carry product samples with them should be alert to import duties they may be required to pay. In some countries, duties and extensive customs procedures on sample products may be avoided by obtaining an ATA (Admission Temporoire) Carnet.

The ATA Carnet is a standardized international customs document used to obtain duty-free temporary admission of certain goods into the countries that are signatories to the ATA Convention. Under the ATA Convention, commercial and professional travelers may take commercial samples; tools of the trade; advertising material; and cinematographic, audiovisual, medical, scientific, or other professional equipment into member countries temporarily without paying customs duties and taxes or posting a bond at the border of each country to be visited.

The following countries currently participate in the ATA Carnet system: Australia, Austria, Belgium, Bulgaria, Canada (certain professional equipment is not accepted), Cyprus, Czechoslovakia, Denmark, Finland, France, Gibraltar, Greece, Hong Kong, Hungary, Iceland, India (commercial samples only), Iran, Ireland, Israel, Italy, Ivory Coast, Japan, Luxembourg, Mauritius, Netherlands, New Zealand, Norway, Poland, Portugal, Romania, Senegal, Singapore, Sri Lanka (certain professional equipment not accepted), South Africa, South Korea, Spain, Sweden, Switzerland, Turkey, United Kingdom, United States, Germany, and Yugoslavia.

Applications for carnets should be made to the same organization. A fee is charged, depending on the value of the goods to be covered. A bond, letter of credit, or bank guaranty of 40 percent of the value of the goods is also required to cover duties and taxes that would be due if goods imported into a foreign country by carnet were not reexported and the duties were not paid by the carnet holder. The carnets generally are valid for 12 months. Contact U.S.

CULTURAL FACTORS

Business executives who hope to profit from their travel should learn about the history, culture, and customs of the countries to be visited. Flexibility and cultural adaptation should be the guiding principles for traveling abroad on business. Business manners and methods, religious customs, dietary practices, humor, and acceptable dress vary widely from country to country. For example, consider the following:

Never touch the head of a Thai or pass an object over it; the head is considered sacred in Thailand.

Avoid using triangular shapes in Hong Kong, Korea, and Taiwan; the triangle is considered a negative shape.

The number 7 is considered bad luck in Kenya and good luck in Czechoslovakia, and it has magical connotations in Benin. The number 10 is bad luck in Korea, and 4 means death in Japan.

Red is a positive color in Denmark, but it represents witchcraft and death in many African countries.

A nod means no in Bulgaria, and shaking the head from side to side means yes.

The "okay" sign commonly used in the United States and the United Kingdom (thumb and index finger forming a circle and the other fingers raised) means zero in France, is a symbol for money in Japan, and carries a vulgar connotation in Brazil.

The use of a palm-up hand and moving index finger signals "come here" in the United States and in some other countries, but it is considered vulgar in others.

In Ethiopia, repeatedly opening and closing the palm-down hand means "come here."

Understanding and heeding cultural variables such as these is critical to success in international business travel and in international business itself. Lack of familiarity with the business practices, social customs, and etiquette of a country can weaken a company's position in the market, prevent it from accomplishing its objectives, and ultimately lead to failure.

Some of the cultural distinctions that firms most often face include differences in business styles, attitudes toward development of business relationships, attitudes toward punctuality, negotiating styles, gift-giving customs, greetings, significance of gestures, meanings of colors and numbers, and customs regarding titles.

Firms must pay close attention to different styles of doing business and the degree of importance placed on developing business relationships. In some countries, business people have a very direct style, while in others they are much more subtle in style and value the personal relationship more than most of us do in business. For example, in the Middle East, engaging in small talk before engaging in business is standard practice.

Attitudes toward punctuality vary greatly from one culture to another and, if misunderstood, can cause confusion and misunderstanding. Romanians, Japanese, and Germans are very punctual, whereas people in many of the Latin countries have a more relaxed attitude toward time. The Japanese consider it rude to be late for a business meeting, but acceptable, even fashionable, to be late for a social occasion. In Guatemala, on the other hand, one might arrive anytime from 10 minutes early to 45 minutes late for a luncheon appointment.

When cultural lines are being crossed, something as simple as a greeting can be misunderstood. Traditional greetings may be a handshake, a hug, a nose rub, a kiss, placing the hands in praying position, or various other gestures. Lack of awareness concerning the country's accepted form of greeting can lead to awkward encounters.

People around the world use body movements and gestures to convey specific messages. Sometimes the same gestures have very different meanings, however. Misunderstanding over gestures is a common occurrence in cross-cultural communication, and misinterpretation along these lines can lead to business complications and social embarrassment.

Proper use of names and titles is often a source of confusion in international business relations. In many countries (including the United Kingdom, France, and Denmark) it is appropriate to use titles until use of first names is suggested. First names are seldom used when doing business in Germany. Visiting business people should use the surname preceded by the title. Titles such as "Herr Direktor" are sometimes used to indicate prestige, status, and rank. Thais, on the other hand, address one other by first names and reserve last names for very formal occasions and written communications. In Belgium it is important to address French-speaking business contacts as "Monsieur" or "Madame," while Dutch-speaking contacts should be addressed as "Mr." or "Mrs." To confuse the two is a great insult.

Customs concerning gift giving are extremely important to understand. In some cultures gifts are expected and failure to present them is considered an insult, whereas in other countries offering a gift is considered offensive. Business executives also need to know when to present gifts - on the initial visit or afterwards; where to present gifts - in public or private; what type of gift to present; what color it should be; and how many to present.

Gift giving is an important part of doing business in Japan, where gifts are usually exchanged at the first meeting. In sharp contrast, gifts are rarely exchanged in Germany and are usually not appropriate. Gift giving is not a normal custom in Belgium or the United Kingdom either, although in both countries, flowers are a suitable gift when invited to someone's home.

Customs concerning the exchange of business cards vary, too. Although this point seems of minor importance, observing a country's customs for card giving is a key part of business protocol. In Japan, for example, the Western practice of accepting a business card and pocketing it immediately is considered rude. The proper approach is to carefully look at the card after accepting it, observe the title and organization, acknowledge with a nod that the information has been digested, and perhaps make a relevant comment or ask a polite question.

Negotiating - a complex process even between parties from the same nation - is even more complicated in international transactions because of the added chance of misunderstandings stemming from cultural differences. It is essential to understand the importance of rank in the other country; to know who the decision makers are; to be familiar with the business style of the foreign company; and to understand the nature of agreements in the country, the significance of gestures, and negotiating etiquette.

It is important to acquire, through reading or training, a basic knowledge of the business culture, management attitudes, business methods, and consumer habits of the country being visited. This does not mean that the traveler must go native when conducting business abroad. It does mean that the traveler should be sensitive to the customs and business procedures of the country being visited.

19. Special Free Bonuses (download links are provided)

a. Excel Financial Projections Creator - simply type in your business' details and assumptions and it will automatically produce a comprehensive set of financial projections for your specific business, including: Start-Up Expenses, Projected Balance Sheet, Projected Cash Flow Statement, Financial Ratios Analysis, Projected Profit and Loss Statement, Break Even Analysis, and many more.

Copy the following link to your browser and save the file to your PC:

http://www.bizmove.com/bp/projections.xlsx

b. Detailed guide that will walk you step by step and show you exactly how to effectively use the above Excel Financial Projections Creator.

Copy the following link to your browser and save the file to your PC:

http://www.bizmove.com/bp/projections-guide.doc

c. How to Improve Your Leadership and Management Skills (eBook) - Discover powerful strategies to motivate and inspire your people to bring out the best in them. Be the boss people want to give 200 percent for.

Copy the following link to your browser and save the file to your PC:

http://www.bizmove.com/bp/leadership.pdf

d. Small Business Management: Essential Ingredients for Success (eBook) - Learn effective business management tricks, secrets and shortcuts to make your business a success.

Copy the following link to your browser and save the file to your PC:

http://www.bizmove.com/bp/management.pdf

www.ingramcontent.com/pod-product-compliance
Lightning Source LLC
Chambersburg PA
CBHW060856170526
45158CB00001B/376